E·I·U
The Economist Intelligence Unit

RESEARCH REPORT

The pros and cons of EMU

by David Currie

Written with the support of:

ABN-Amro Hoare Govett
Banca Nazionale del Lavoro
Deutsche Morgan Grenfell
Kleinwort Benson Group
Peregrine Investments Holdings
Prudential
Reuters
J Rothschild Assurance
N M Rothschild & Sons
Schroders

The Economist Intelligence Unit
15 Regent Street, London SW1Y 4LR
United Kingdom

The Economist Intelligence Unit

The Economist Intelligence Unit is a specialist publisher serving companies establishing and managing operations across national borders. For over 40 years it has been a source of information on business developments, economic and political trends, government regulations and corporate practice worldwide.

The EIU delivers its information in four ways: through subscription products ranging from newsletters to annual reference works; through specific research reports, whether for general release or for particular clients; through electronic publishing; and by organising conferences and roundtables. The firm is a member of The Economist Group.

London
The Economist Intelligence Unit
15 Regent Street
London
SW1Y 4LR
United Kingdom
Tel: (44.171) 830 1000
Fax: (44.171) 499 9767

New York
The Economist Intelligence Unit
The Economist Building
111 West 57th Street
New York
NY 10019, USA
Tel: (1.212) 554 0600
Fax: (1.212) 586 1181/2

Hong Kong
The Economist Intelligence Unit
25/F, Dah Sing Financial Centre
108 Gloucester Road
Wanchai
Hong Kong
Tel: (852) 2802 7288
Fax: (852) 2802 7638

Electronic delivery

EIU Electronic
New York: Lou Celi or Lisa Hennessey Tel: (1.212) 554 0600 Fax: (1.212) 586 0248
London: Moya Veitch Tel: (44.171) 830 1007 Fax: (44.171) 830 1023

This publication is available on the following electronic and other media:

Online databases

FT Profile (UK)
Tel: (44.171) 825 8000

M.A.I.D/Profound (UK)
Tel: (44.171) 930 6900

MarkIntel (USA)
Tel: (1.617) 345 5933

Copyright

ISBN 0 85058 922 3

Symbols for tables

"n/a" means not available; "–" means not applicable

Printed by the Charlesworth Group, 254 Deighton Road, Huddersfield, UK

January 20, 1997

Contents

List of figures

**This report is dedicated
to the memory of Nico Colchester**

Preface

In working towards implementation of economic and monetary union and a single currency, the European Union and its member states—both those committed to EMU should they qualify, and those which have yet to make up their minds—will be taking major decisions. Few question that the issue is a vital one, both economically and politically.

This report has been sponsored by a group of leading financial institutions which feel that the debate on this vital issue has not been sufficiently well-informed. In some countries within the EU, the debate has been lopsided and incomplete. In others, including the United Kingdom, there has been extensive debate, but too little attempt to shed light on the key issues that underlie this momentous decision.

The aim of the report is to analyse the key issues surrounding EMU in as objective and dispassionate a manner as possible. It seeks to disentangle the various elements of the debate in such a way as to allow readers to make up their own minds about the issues. It tries not to sit on the fence, but to set out clearly and fairly the basis of the many complicated arguments involved. The report's aim is not to push one particular line, but to provide the basis for a better informed and reasoned debate on this vital issue, in the UK and elsewhere.

To this end, on behalf of the sponsors, Nico Colchester of the Economist Intelligence Unit commissioned David Currie, Professor of Economics at London Business School, and formerly an adviser to the UK's chancellor of the exchequer, to write this report. In the course of its preparation, Nico tragically and unexpectedly died. Had he lived, he would have made a major input to the shape and promotion of the report, and this was sadly missed. Instead we were fortunate that Clive Crook was willing to step into this role, despite the many other claims on his time as Deputy Editor of *The Economist*.

In October 1996, David Currie was appointed a working Labour peer in the House of Lords, in addition to his continued full-time academic appointment at London Business School. This development was as complete a surprise to him as it was to the EIU and the sponsors. Coming as it did in the middle of his work on the report, we were concerned that it should not compromise the report's objectivity and impartiality. David Currie himself was determined not to allow either this project or his other academic work to be influenced, and he undertook to deliver fully the impartiality required by the original brief for this project.

On behalf of the sponsors, I can say that we are convinced that he has achieved this admirably. We are very happy to be associated with this report as an informed, objective and dispassionate analysis of the issues surrounding EMU. The views expressed in the report are, however, the author's, and do not necessarily reflect the different positions of the individual sponsors, the EIU and *The Economist.*

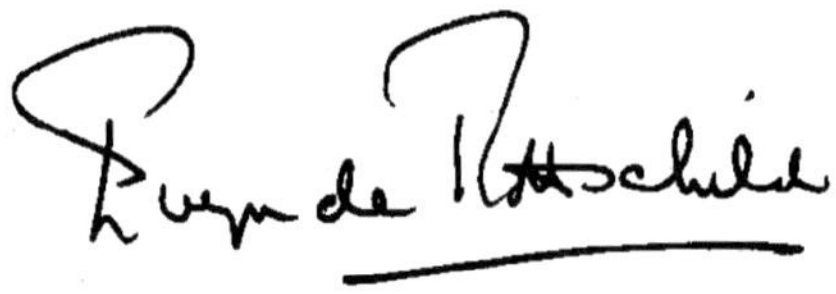

Sir Evelyn de Rothschild

Summary

Europe has embarked on an extraordinary undertaking: to create a single European currency. Although the Maastricht treaty committed the European Union to the goal of economic and monetary union (EMU) several years ago, debate over all aspects of the matter continues to rage. What kind of project is it: an economic initiative, intended to derive the greatest benefits from Europe's single market, or a broader political idea, leading to closer integration of Europe's governments? Can the Maastricht plan, subsequently modified, be made to work? And supposing it can, will Europe's new currency, the euro, prove to be a blessing or a curse? (Chapter 1)

Monetary union and national sovereignty

For many people, friends and foes of EMU alike, the single currency points inescapably to closer political union. Both the history of other single currency areas and the commitment of a number of key EU member governments to further political integration suggest that over time, EMU will indeed favour federalism. *De facto* monetary unions linking states of dissimilar size and power (like that of Belgium and Luxembourg today) have not been uncommon. However, there has so far never been one enduring monetary union of strong independent states.

Yet in theory there seems no compelling economic reason why this should be so. The extent of "political union" remains essentially a matter of political choice. European countries have already moved a good way down the road to federalism by ceding powers to EU institutions. Adopting the single currency means, by definition, surrendering national control over monetary policy, but no further loss of national sovereignty would necessarily be bound to follow. Europe's governments may well choose that course, and the December 1996 agreement of a majority of governments to accept limits on their fiscal deficits may well be a sign of more centralisation to come. Or they may choose otherwise. Participating in EMU does not pre-ordain that decision. Some argue that the decision has already been taken, and that the EU is headed firmly on an undesirable centralising route; others see the future as much more open; others still see greater political union as desirable, creating a stronger and more effective EU. (Chapter 2)

EMU's workability

That being so, the case for or against EMU requires a careful analysis of the economic pros and cons. Critics of the single currency, citing the chaos that engulfed the European exchange rate mechanism in 1992 and 1993, argue that monetary union is simply unworkable. This is mistaken. EMU is partly a response to the flaws of the earlier system, which sought monetary stability through cooperation among central banks (putting the regime at the mercy of the foreign exchange markets) rather than by means of a single currency (which is not exposed to that hazard).

Another objection to the Maastricht blueprint is that EMU will face severe transitional difficulties: so severe, perhaps, that the project would better be abandoned. This is a stronger point. There will indeed be difficulties of various sorts between now and 1998 (when governments will decide which countries are to participate), between 1998 and 1999 (when members' exchange rates are to be "irrevocably" fixed), and between 1999 and 2002 (when national currencies are finally withdrawn from circulation).

A further set of key questions about the workability of EMU arises from the economic adjustment that will be needed between countries through labour mobility or adjustment of wage levels. Labour market flexibility will greatly help with the implementation of EMU, but is necessary, with or without EMU, for a successful and dynamic European economy.

But none of these difficulties is insuperable. EMU can be built, provided governments are willing to grapple with the underlying problems. (Chapter 3)

Implications for macroeconomic policy

EMU will have great implications for the conduct of macroeconomic policy in Europe. Because of the attention that has been paid to the design of the European Central Bank (ECB), the euro countries are likely to enjoy low and stable inflation, to the benefit of consumers, investors and businesses. For many, particularly in those countries that historically have been prone to high inflation, this is a great gain, sufficient perhaps to justify the entire project. But the drawback is that governments will lose their ability to respond to economic circumstances by changing their own national interest rates, or by letting their own currencies depreciate.

In many countries this freedom has been greatly abused: the cost of surrendering it is therefore smaller than might be thought. But in countries where monetary policy has been well conducted, the cost is significant. The balance of cost and benefit will depend partly on how much flexibility is allowed in the conduct of national fiscal policies. Some fear that EMU will encourage profligate countries to borrow excessively, a fear compounded by concerns over unfunded government pension liabilities in Europe. But there are signs that the Maastricht design is encouraging a move to low public deficits and prudent fiscal policies. (Chapter 4)

The single market reborn

For businesses, the chief direct benefit of the single currency is that it will remove some of the costs and uncertainties associated with intra-European trade. Companies often have to take long-term exchange rate positions (for instance, in deciding where to locate). Such positions can be hedged, but only at a cost. In any case it does not make sense to hedge fully. By reducing these costs and uncertainties, EMU will promote trade and investment, speeding the rationalisation of industry across Europe. The gains from this will be passed on to Europe's consumers. In other respects, EMU could hinder business: for instance, by encouraging Europe-wide comparisons in wage negotiations, or by promoting further social legislation as part of a broader trend towards federalism. These dangers need to be guarded against. If they are, the net benefits for Europe's businesses could be substantial. (Chapter 5)

The effects on finance

Europe's banks and securities businesses are a special case. In banking, national markets have been segmented by regulation and separate currencies. The single currency will intensify pressures for a restructuring of European banking. The same is true of financial markets more generally. Already the mere prospect of EMU has stimulated intense competition between financial centres in Europe, notably Frankfurt, London and Paris. The development of large markets in euro-denominated securities raises the stakes. Banks, other financial institutions and exchanges all need to prepare carefully for the transition to the euro if they are not to lose out. This is true regardless of whether they are based in a participating member state. If financial institutions are well prepared, being based in an "out" need not be a serious disadvantage. (Chapters 6 and 7)

The future of the EU

EMU will also have profound implications for the development of the EU as a whole. There may be deepening divisions between "ins" and "outs" (some of which could more accurately be described as "pre-ins"). If "outs" and "pre-ins" see their privileges within the single market eroded, the cost could be great, but this need not, and should not, be allowed to happen. A greater risk is that EMU will delay further enlargement of the EU. On the other hand, if EMU works well it could revive the momentum of the single-market programme, and ease negotiation of the different issues involved in enlargement.

EMU, then, will have both good and bad effects. The balance of pros and cons is complicated, uncertain and unavoidably subjective. Indeed, we can foresee a number of outcomes for EMU (which we set out more fully in the report as four plausible scenarios). It remains a possibility (though decreasingly likely as the January 1, 1999 deadline looms) that the EMU process will be deferred. If deferment happens in a negative way, it is easy to see how it could lead to a loss of political confidence in the EU and a collapse into bitter international acrimony. That could easily divide Europe, preventing the EU from addressing its other crucial policy issues, including tackling structural rigidities in the European economy, issues of EU governance, and the question of enlargement to the east. But if deferment of EMU happens in a constructive, harmonious way, that could well allow the EU to tackle vigorously these other policy agendas. The EMU agenda could be replaced by a "competitiveness comes first" programme, resulting in renewed growth and dynamism in the European economy.

In the more likely event that EMU proceeds, it may work badly or well. Joblessness could rise further, governments could borrow excessively, and EMU could become characterised as deflationary and debt-ridden. In time, a political backlash could develop against the euro. In these circumstances, there could well be a reluctance to address liberalisation and enlargement, and Europe could become more divided.

But if these dangers could be avoided, the greater competition and integration that the single currency would bring would boost the single market and promote efficiency and growth in the European economy. It is possible to see how confidence in the EU would rise, making it easier to tackle the other key agendas of liberalisation, governance and enlargement.

Conclusion

The crucial point is this: none of these scenarios is impossible. We do expect EMU to happen. Far more tentatively, we expect it to be a partial success, though not necessarily for all its members. What is clear, however, and what has been insufficiently understood, is that going forward with EMU does not condemn Europe to failure, nor guarantee its success. And the same goes for abandoning the single currency project. The pros and cons are too finely balanced to allow any such conclusion. Regardless of whether EMU happens, everything will depend on the wisdom of choices that governments have yet to make. (Chapter 8)

Notes

Chapter 1 Introduction

Why EMU excites strong emotions

Antis

The debate over economic and monetary union in Europe has polarised opinion to an extraordinary degree. For many who oppose the single currency, EMU is not merely an ill-advised undertaking, but a disastrous one: a stride further along the road to a European superstate that will submerge the individuality of the European nations in an unwieldy federation, hobbled by bureaucracy, commanding little popular support and imposing a crippling burden of regulatory and other costs on Europe's economies. Opponents also see it as a distraction from the two most urgent tasks currently facing the EU: completion of the single market and enlargement of the Union to the east (which is crucial to provide stability to an area that will otherwise lack it). Many argue that EMU is likely to prove unworkable; others believe that it will impair Europe's economic performance, worsening the region's unemployment, adding to disparities in incomes and dividing Europe dangerously between "ins" and "outs". Some even fear that the centralising tendencies of EMU will awaken Europe's dormant nationalisms, which twice this century have led to world war.

Pros

Many advocates of EMU reply in kind. They see not only a chance to achieve worthwhile economic benefits, but also a fleeting opportunity to grasp an historic prize. They regard EMU as essential to creating a stronger EU, with greater economic, political and social cohesion. Without it, they say, the reality of the single market will not be achieved and Europe's economies will remain divided and weak, unable to compete internationally either with the low-wage econ- omies of Asia or with the large, integrated, high-wage economy of the USA. Europe's relative decline, measured both by economic performance and by political power, would accelerate. A strong EU, it is argued, offers the best hope for helping the former communist-bloc countries: closer integration among the current EU members helps, not hinders, the prospects for enlargement. Only a stronger and more integrated Europe will be able to exercise leadership on the global issues facing the world economy.

The narrower UK perspective

What is at stake in the argument seems no less momentous when viewed from a narrower UK perspective. Opponents of British participation argue for steering well clear of an ill-considered experiment that will impose a severe competitive handicap on the countries that participate. By standing aside, the UK will avoid the instabilities that the single currency will cause, and will keep its present competitive edge. In particular, the sceptics say, the City of London will flourish best outside the single-currency area, thereby unencumbered by excessive regulation. Taking a broader view, some opponents of EMU argue that the UK's future lies not in economic alliance with Europe, weighed down by sclerotic and over-regulated economies, but rather with the dynamic market economies of the Pacific Rim. The UK should be thinking not at a European level but globally about its economic and political place in the world.

Advocates of the UK's participation say this is all wrong. If the country stands aside it will be marginalised in its most important market, with consequences that go far beyond trade with the EU. The UK would henceforth be a much less attractive location for inward direct investment from other parts of the world. This is a particular concern since such investment has played a crucial role in transforming the UK's industrial performance. They also worry for the future of the City if the UK remains outside EMU. More generally, they see the UK's future as part of Europe, and fear that a decision to stand aside will merely repeat the pattern of the past, when the country repeatedly chose to play no part in planning Europe's future, only to be forced in time to follow the course charted by others.

It ought to be clear, at least, that issues as big as these require the most careful consideration. The questions involved are complex, and reasonable people may well disagree about them. Yet all too often the debate on EMU is conducted in terms of headlines and slogans, from entrenched and unalterable positions, often without regard for the facts.

Aims and structure of the report

The aim of this report is to analyse the issues surrounding EMU in as objective and dispassionate a manner as possible, and to disentangle the various elements of the debate in such a way that readers may make up their own minds. We do this not by sitting on the fence: on each point, we will make it clear where our assessment of the arguments leads us. But if we succeed in setting out the arguments clearly and fairly, readers will more easily be able to make up their own mind, and may well reach a different conclusion. In other words our purpose is not to push any particular line, but to provide the basis for a better informed and more reasoned debate on this vital matter. The structure of the report is as follows.

What history teaches

The next two chapters provide some essential historical background. First, in Chapter 2, we examine through the lens of economic history the issue that is central to the EMU debate: in the past, how far have choices about monetary union foreclosed choices about political sovereignty? Then, in Chapter 3, we review the history of Europe's single-currency project so far, and examine some of the transitional difficulties that have yet to be faced. This sheds a revealing light on the blueprint for EMU that emerged in the Maastricht treaty, and on many of the arguments that are now made for and against that plan.

Macro- and microeconomic issues

Chapters 4-7 form the core of the report. They examine the economic arguments for and against the single currency, sector by sector. Chapter 4 considers the macroeconomic arguments that have dominated the debate up to now.

The first question examined there follows directly from the issue of sovereignty discussed in Chapter 2: does monetary union oblige governments to surrender control of fiscal policy to a central authority? This chapter goes on to ask whether EMU members, lacking national control of interest rates, could cope adequately with economic shocks; whether the single currency would bring gains in terms of lower inflation, and/or costs in terms of higher unemployment, Europe-wide; and what the other macroeconomic costs and benefits of EMU would be. Then Chapters 5-7 shift to microeconomics, looking in turn at the effect that the single currency would have on non-financial businesses (Chapter 5), on banks (Chapter 6), and finally on securities markets and investment funds (Chapter 7).

Impact on Europe

Chapter 8 tries to draw the strands of these arguments together. It considers, in the light of what we have learned so far about the sectoral costs and benefits of the single currency, some of the broader issues raised in the EMU debate. In particular, it examines the development of the EU under the influence of the single currency: how the relationship between members and non-members of the single currency would evolve, what the implications for enlargement might be, and how Europe's economic and political relations with the rest of the world might change. Then, in an effort to crystallise the principal issues, while recognising the uncertainties that are bound to make a choice of this kind extremely difficult, it discusses four possible futures.

Plausible scenarios

Two of these scenarios assume that the single-currency project goes through: one describes what a successful future for Europe with a single currency could look like; another describes a much worse outcome, in which the drawbacks of the single currency overwhelm the hoped-for benefits. The other two scenarios, in contrast, assume that the EMU project is either abandoned or indefinitely delayed. Again, one of these describes a successful future, this time without a single currency, and the other describes an unsuccessful future, in which the fears of the most enthusiastic advocates of EMU, should the single currency not happen, come to pass.

We argue, such are the uncertainties, that all four of these scenarios must be regarded as feasible. The question is: which is the most probable, and what might be the costs of backing the wrong options? More tentatively than elsewhere in the report (because we hope that readers by now are equipped to make up their own minds), we offer a view on that too. But our main contention is that this weighing of plausible futures is the right way to think about the great choice currently facing Europe. It is an approach to be contrasted with the present debate, in which one kind of specious certainty joins battle with another. A more intelligent debate is urgently needed. Our hope is that the analysis in the pages that follow will help in that task.

Chapter 2 Monetary union and national sovereignty

In this chapter we examine the connection between monetary union and national sovereignty. Does a single currency bring with it a major and irrevocable loss of national sovereignty? Or does it represent merely the loss of a symbol of national sovereignty, long since eroded by other forces? To answer these crucial questions, we look at EMU in an historical and international setting.

Money and the state

EMU affects a crucial aspect of a country's independence: control of a national currency. Over the centuries, the nation's currency, bearing the head of the king, queen or president, has everywhere symbolised national autonomy. Because of this history, money—together with armies and pageantry—is one of the most potent symbols of nations. Abandoning the national currency in favour of the proposed euro appears to many to signify a loss of nationhood.

Not everybody would regard such a loss as a bad thing. Many advocates of closer European integration see the weakening of the nation state in Europe as a positive development, despite its undoubted contribution to economic and industrial development. Reducing the powers of the nation state and binding European states together makes it less likely, it is argued, that European nationalism will tear Europe apart in the way that has happened twice in the past century in two world wars. This was the vision that inspired the European Community's early architects, and above all Jean Monnet. This vision also underlies Chancellor Helmut Kohl's wish to pursue the political dimensions of European integration in parallel with the EMU project. Enthusiastic federalists therefore often see the move to a single currency as another important step towards a more united Europe.

However, according to another way of thinking (shared by Kenneth Clarke, the UK's chancellor of the exchequer), the link between money and sovereignty is not so clear. On this view, adopting a common currency is an important technical development that enhances economic integration, but it need not bring with it a loss of sovereignty. If this is correct, it would follow that the case for or against a single currency depends on its direct costs and benefits, not on the broader political case for or against a federal Europe.

It is crucial to resolve this question, for it is fundamental to any appraisal of EMU. If monetary union implies federalism, then the calculation of direct costs and benefits is unlikely to be decisive, unless the balance is very large: a minor net cost or benefit is unlikely to outweigh the political considerations of sovereignty versus federalism. But if federalism does not follow automatically from

EMU, then the economic balance sheet could be decisive, even if the net balance is quite small.

In this chapter, we aim to clarify the linkage between a single currency and federalism by looking at the historical evidence. Our broad conclusions are as follows.

- There is a clear tendency for sovereign or federal structures to be linked with a single currency; indeed, there are no examples of single-currency areas that do not involve the sharing of sovereignty between their constituent parts. This suggests EMU will favour European federalism.

- This is, at best, a long-run tendency: there are plenty of examples of single-currency areas where the pooling of national powers came a long while after the creation of the single currency.

- EU member states have already pooled a great deal of powers, so that the EU is best described as a loose federation or confederation. Whether EMU requires a great deal of further pooling of national powers and consequent loss of national sovereignty is much less clear. More generally, the degree of federation is a matter of choice: the EU could, if its members chose, adopt a centralised form of federation, as in Germany, or it could adopt a looser form, as in Switzerland.

Legal tender and seigniorage

Money's three key functions

In the past, all manner of things have performed the three key functions of money: as medium of exchange, unit of account and store of value. What is used at any particular time and place depends on what suits the parties on each side of the transaction. Any good which has scarcity value, which retains that value, and which is divisible and somewhat standardisable can play the role of money. Grain, shells, metals, and more recently cigarettes (in prisoner-of-war camps) have all served as money. In all these cases, what would play the role of money was decided in the market: particular commodities could be used in transactions only if both buyer and seller agreed.

Usually, however, money is associated with the power of the state. The state uses its legal and political authority to require that the money that it issues is acceptable to sellers; the money is thus defined as *legal tender*, and the state enjoys a unique position as the monopoly supplier of money.

This arrangement, ultimately based on the power of the state, has advantages. By ensuring that its money is universally acceptable within the boundaries of the state, the government makes that money much more efficient in use: sellers will accept it, confident that it will be accepted again when they come to buy. And the state can use its powers to guarantee the quality of its money, traditionally by guaranteeing its gold or silver content and more recently by providing the assurance of a responsible monetary policy that does not result in inflation.

At the same time, the state derives a fiscal benefit from its monopoly position as the supplier of money. Merely by issuing more money, which in itself costs almost nothing, the state is able to purchase more goods and services. In periods of rising prices, when more money is needed to transact business, the issue of additional cash yields appreciable revenues to the state. These are called seigniorage.

Inflation: the hidden tax

Even when paper money was linked to gold, seigniorage still arose from the fractional reserve system. With the abandonment of the gold system, the scope for the government to generate seigniorage was greatly increased. Creating more money gave the state extra purchasing power, while at the same time it pushed up prices. Seigniorage was renamed the "inflation tax", and Milton Friedman, the founder of modern monetarism, argued against this form of "taxation without representation".

For some countries, seigniorage has been a very important source of government revenue, providing an important alternative to overt taxation. In Greece it used to account for revenues equivalent to some 5% of GDP a decade or more ago. In Italy the corresponding figure was a lower, but still sizeable, 3%, before the treasury and central bank "divorced" in 1981. But this reflects the then underdeveloped or repressed nature of the financial systems of these countries.

In the typical economy with developed and sophisticated financial systems, seigniorage has shrunk appreciably. This is because in a more sophisticated system investors have many interest-yielding alternatives to cash, and therefore prefer to hold assets other than non-interest-bearing cash. And since it is the issue of non-interest-bearing cash that yields seigniorage to the government, this source of revenue is quite small in well-developed financial systems, especially when inflation is low. (For the UK, for example, it is now typically less than 0.25% of GDP, or £1.5bn per year.) As a source of government revenue, it is largely irrelevant. The UK government, in common with most others in developed economies, relies on debt rather than money to finance its deficits. Unlike seigniorage, this form of finance pays interest, so it does not represent a hidden tax.

In the modern, globally integrated world, seigniorage has an international aspect. More open financial markets give investors wider international choice, reducing their need to hold the national currency, and thereby cutting further the importance of seigniorage. At the same time, countries with internationally dominant currencies, such as the USA, are able to issue large amounts of debt denominated in their domestic currency to international investors. Other, less privileged countries find that their capacity to borrow in their domestic currency is rather limited. This is for a very good reason: with a large stock of debt denominated in domestic currency but held internationally, the country and/or government can benefit substantially from a devaluation, which cuts the value of that debt to foreigners and the costs of debt service to the country. Because of this, international investors are reluctant to lend on a large scale except to countries where the prospect of devaluation is minimal.

Over the past decade, the exception has been the USA. Since the dollar is so widely used for trading purposes, there has been a substantial international demand for dollars, despite the risk that the dollar could fall in value, deliberately or otherwise, because of a loose US monetary policy. This has enabled the

USA to run its very large current-account deficits throughout the 1980s, largely through Japanese finance. Because of the fall in the dollar since 1985, these Japanese investments have shown a very low, even negative, return, to the detriment of the Japanese but to the advantage of the USA. A key reason why this has been possible is the general use of the US dollar for trading purposes (its so-called vehicle currency use). Were the new euro to displace the dollar in this role, then this advantage to the USA would be reduced. The rise of the euro could help the European economy, but at the expense of the USA. How important this modern seigniorage effect will be depends particularly on how the Asian economies view EMU and the euro. We return to these questions later in this report.

In time of war

The shrinkage of domestic seigniorage in developed economies might suggest that the link between money and the nation state is largely a symbol, albeit a potent one, and of little practical importance. This, however, may be a hasty judgement. Seigniorage has been a very important source of government finance in the past in times of national emergency. This has been particularly the case in times of war: inflationary money finance has been used many times in wartime to meet the unexpected spending on the military.

The UK broke the link between the pound and gold in 1914 when it became clear that its gold reserves were insufficient to finance the war. This allowed budget deficits to be financed by money issues. The result was a sharp rise in prices, but in the circumstances this was preferable to the alternative: being unable to prosecute the war. (The link to gold was re-established only in 1925, and then only for a brief period up to 1931.) In the Second World War, there was less recourse to money financing because of a highly effective programme to encourage (or perhaps force) savings to finance the war effort. Prices therefore rose less. However, had the extra savings not been forthcoming, there is no doubt that the inflation tax would have played a crucial role. Money financing also played an important part in financing Germany's war effort (memories of hyperinflation in the 1920s notwithstanding).

Perhaps the most striking example of inflationary finance of wars and of the importance of money to nation states (both actual and aspirant) came in the American civil war. The tax-raising powers of the Southern Confederacy forces

Figure 2.1
UK inflation, 1900-50

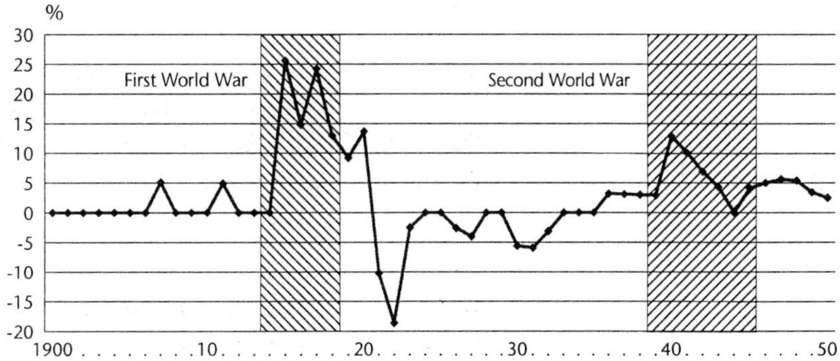

Source: The Economist, *Economic Statistics 1900-1983*, 1985.

were weak, and the states turned to the printing press. Prices in terms of the Southern currency rose several hundred per cent in crucial stages of the war. When the Northern troops captured the key Southern printing press, it proved a decisive moment in the war. Not only did inflation stop dead in its tracks (proving that money causes inflation), but the Southern war effort was crucially undermined. The printing press was as important a military target as the army camps.

The use of money financing is much more circumscribed in today's conditions of highly integrated international capital markets. If the UK government, say, resorted to the printing press, this could easily precipitate a major flight from the currency, and a scramble to look for alternative money such as the dollar—or the euro. But in extreme conditions of national emergency, money financing would not be impossible. It would probably require the imposition of exchange controls, limiting the capacity of investors to switch to other currencies. This would disrupt financial markets and work imperfectly at best. As a routine way to finance spending, such measures are out of the question. But to tackle a grave national emergency, such as invasion or war, they may be both acceptable and practical. Without an independent currency, such measures would be well nigh impossible. The prospect of war or invasion may seem slight within the EU, but some would argue that the history of the last century makes it wise to retain this emergency policy option.

One money, one nation?

The importance of seigniorage in the past raises the question as to whether monetary and political jurisdictions have, as a matter of historical fact, ever differed, and if so under what circumstances. If these jurisdictions have always been identical, then one might well argue on that count alone that EMU is a doomed venture, or else that it must bring in its wake a federal Europe in which the current nation states are subordinate.

In modern times, the link between currencies and nations has been a strong one. Only in a few instances, usually of weakened national power, has it been broken. Moreover, the imposition of a currency on a country has often been an important part of suppressing its nationhood.

Once free, adopt your own currency

One of the very early acts of the new countries that sprang from the ashes of the ruined Soviet empire was to design a new currency. Significantly, countries that lacked a secure basis for independence subsequently re-established their link to the rouble, perceived as a powerful symbol of their dependence on Russia. The resolution of the American civil war went together with the suppression of the Southern Confederacy currency, and the general circulation of the Northern currency was, among other things, an important symbol of Northern supremacy.

It is striking that people continue to use their national currency (rather than abandon it for another) even in extreme circumstances. In Germany in the hyperinflation of 1922-23, when the *monthly* rate of inflation reached nearly 30,000%, people carried on using German money. To be sure, at such times other currencies circulate alongside the national money. The dollar has often been a dual currency, widely acceptable around the world; today it functions as a second currency in Russia and Mexico, and in many other unstable economies. But this only confirms the point that the widespread use of a foreign currency in domestic transactions is usually a sign that the state concerned is very weak.

To delegate is not to surrender

Historical evidence could therefore be interpreted as suggesting that, in giving up their individual national currencies, European countries entering EMU will be relinquishing an important part of their sovereignty. Against this, however, note the fundamental distinction between delegating powers and surrendering sovereignty. Delegated powers can be taken back; surrendered powers cannot. Delegation does not erode sovereignty, which may be reasserted at any time. Some might argue that the European countries entering EMU are merely delegating their monetary powers and can take them back at any time if they wish to. Other might counter that this argument verges on sophistry, not least because if the market regarded EMU as reversible, the euro would hardly be an attractive currency.

What is the reality?

International treaties such as the Treaty of Rome and Maastricht lack provision for signatories to reclaim powers given to European institutions. But a country set on withdrawing from the European treaties could not be stopped in practice. Ultimately nationhood is determined by political and social consciousness and cohesion. While external political and military force could, in principle, force the UK or any other country to remain part of a federal Europe against its wishes, this possibility is inconceivable in the conditions of modern Europe. A separation would be like an amicable divorce: negotiated with regrets.

What will keep European countries in the EU will be a political, economic and social calculation of the benefits and costs of breaking away. The greater the degree of integration, the more costly a divorce would be. This raises the question of just how great the costs of breaking away from EMU would be in practice, once a country has joined.

Would divorce be affordable?

At one level, these costs would not be large. If the UK, say, had joined EMU, and the pound had disappeared, a future English nationalist party (or any other nationalist movement in Europe) elected to power on a wave of anti-European sentiment could conceivably reissue the pound (perhaps at the exchange rate of 10 euros to the pound, to emphasise the pound's superiority); re-staff the Bank of England to oversee the UK's independent monetary policy; and re-establish the pound, not the euro, as legal tender.

This would be a breach of treaty obligations to the UK's European partners, but in the circumstances in which such a course is imaginable, that might count for little. The important test for such a policy would be whether the new currency would be accepted, or whether people would continue to use the euro or switch to the dollar. Again, in the postulated circumstances, this is unlikely to be an insuperable hurdle (provided the new currency looks like the euro and has a simple conversion ratio; otherwise the switch would involve conversion costs that might impede its adoption). This, after all, is the process already undertaken by many of the countries that emerged from the Soviet empire. And as we note a little later, while some monetary unions have prospered and endured, others have come and gone.

So there is nothing irrevocable about EMU. Countries (or regions) could jump ship if they chose. But unless the movement for independence were blindly irrational, whether they would do so would depend on the benefits derived from restoring a national currency. And this in turn would depend on other aspects of economic integration. For instance, if the country had become highly integrated with the rest of Europe, the practical powers of a separate currency might turn out to be quite limited. We explore this question in the following sections.

Internationalisation and the erosion of sovereignty

Capital markets

The last ten years or so have seen a remarkable transformation of capital markets around the world. Two decades ago, they were highly segmented on national lines, with capital controls limiting the freedom of investors to move funds across national boundaries. Even then, the Euromarkets (not to be confused with the new European euro) in dollars, sterling and other currencies provided an important home for offshore investment and a source of finance for funds outside the control of the national authorities. Despite this pool of international liquidity, national markets remained importantly separated from each other, and this gave autonomy to national monetary authorities in the conduct of their monetary policies.

This segmentation has been swept away by three main developments.

- The growth of international liquidity has been enormous, giving greater and greater influence to funds outside the control of the national authorities. This liquidity increasingly undermined the effectiveness of the capital controls that national authorities imposed to limit the free movement of capital.
- Increased liquidity in turn led to the widespread abolition of capital controls and exchange restrictions.
- The trend was further reinforced by the astonishing development of communications technology. The ability to communicate around the world in seconds meant that geography no longer provided any market separation, and the growth of technology has ensured that all parts of the world are integrated into international financial markets: the automatic segmentation of past eras has disappeared.

The consequence has been an increasingly international, interconnected and interdependent world, in which businesses and even individuals have a choice as to which money they use, and in which that choice is increasingly unimportant because of the ease with which funds can be switched from one currency denomination to another. In this world, governments can maintain their independent currency, but only by ensuring that it remains as attractive to hold as its rivals. This constrains the conduct of monetary policy in important ways: monetary freedom goes with strict limits on monetary discretion.

The power of the markets

The most obvious manifestation of these limits is the power of foreign exchange markets. With more than a trillion dollars trading across the foreign exchanges daily, the powers of the markets are manifest. Arbitrage between currencies by footloose international capital means that there are powerful forces bringing the real returns on different currencies into line: thus the so-called *uncovered interest parity* condition suggests that the expected (unhedged) return from holding similar assets denominated in different currencies, taking account of expected future exchange-rate movements, will be brought into line.

There is a straightforward mechanism for this: if the expected return on sterling assets, for example, is lower than that on, say, Deutschmark assets, then the sterling assets will be sold, driving down sterling and generating the expectation of a subsequent appreciation (relative to the path that was expected before). The expected appreciation of sterling against the D-mark adds to the return on holding sterling assets for an overseas investor (and subtracts from the return on holding D-mark assets for a UK investor), and therefore tends to bring the return on sterling assets into line with that on D-mark assets. A sufficient fall in sterling will therefore equalise the return on sterling and D-mark assets.

If the return on sterling and D-mark assets is equalised through financial market integration, does this mean that monetary policy, which operates through the rate of interest, is powerless? The answer to this is no, provided that the exchange rate is free to move. With a fixed exchange rate, high capital mobility removes the autonomy of monetary policy; interest rates, both real and nominal, will be equalised across countries. But with floating rates, high capital mobility merely means that the rate of return on each currency is equalised for each investor, but allows this rate of return to vary across investors in different currency regions.

So suppose that D-mark interest rates are 6% and UK interest rates are 8%, and foreign exchange markets are in equilibrium because they expect sterling to depreciate by 2% a year. Then UK borrowers face an 8% interest rate, whether they borrow in sterling or D-mark; while German borrowers face a 6% rate, irrespective of currency. Floating exchange rates break the inexorable link between interest rates across integrated financial markets. In the long term, a steady 2% depreciation of sterling against the D-mark probably means that UK inflation will be some 2% higher than German inflation, so that real interest rates are equalised. But except in the long run the link between exchange-rate movements and inflation is quite tenuous (as the post-EMS UK experience shows), so that there is ample scope for differences in nominal interest rates to be translated into differences in real interest rates over an extended period.

Why the exchange rate matters

The upshot is that exchange-rate flexibility allows monetary policy to operate effectively at a national level, despite ever more integrated international capital markets. Provided the consequent fall in the exchange rate is accepted, changes in monetary policy can lower both nominal and real interest rates and thereby influence the domestic economy. Moving to EMU means giving up this policy instrument, and is likely to involve a cost. The principal form that this cost will take is in being unable to lower or raise interest rates independently of other countries when domestic conditions require it; this situation will occur when the domestic economy goes into a recession or inflationary boom not shared by other countries in the EMU zone.

Two negative arguments

We return to this issue in the following two chapters. Here we simply note that there are two main grounds on which proponents of EMU can reasonably argue that the benefits of monetary independence are small or even negative.

- An independent monetary policy will offer few advantages if the linkage from the exchange rate to domestic prices is very close: the so-called *law of one price*. This may occur under several different circumstances: if the goods and labour markets of the country in question are highly integrated with those of the other members of the EMU; or if the labour market of the country exhibits a very high degree of real wage resistance, so that price increases are quickly translated into wage increases and then back into further price increases; or if confidence in the domestic currency is low so that pricing and wage setting decisions are made, explicitly or implicitly, in terms of the foreign currency. In each of these circumstances, a fall in the currency will translate quickly into a corresponding rise in prices. In this case, the monetary authorities will be unable to influence real interest rates, except rather briefly, so that the power of monetary policy will be very limited. The experience of the UK after sterling left the exchange-rate mechanism of the European Monetary System (EMS) in 1992 suggests that these conditions are *not* relevant to the UK case, at least at the present time. But the first two conditions may well be relevant to the smaller economies of continental Europe, suggesting that for them the benefits of an independent monetary policy may be limited.

- An independent monetary policy may well be a curse if the freedom to devalue the currency is misused. The case of Italy, for one, demonstrates that countries with structural problems cannot escape them by devaluing their currencies. The same has been true of the UK over the past three decades. In 1966, sterling traded at about DM11; an independent UK monetary policy had allowed this to slip to around DM2.3 in 1996, an average depreciation of nearly 5% a year over 30 years. Monetary freedom has offered little real benefit to the UK; the principal result has been that it has experienced on average nearly 5% more inflation than Germany. Moreover, the UK economy has exhibited greater instability over this same period than any of its major competitors, due to the signal failure, over much of it, to tackle structural rigidities (see Table 2.1). Thus the independent conduct of UK monetary policy has not given greater cyclical stability. Proponents of the practical (rather than symbolic) benefits of monetary independence do not find it easy to explain away this combination of adverse trend and adverse cycle. Arguably the UK has used its monetary freedom to devalue and put off the need for inevitable real adjustments.

To sum up, the European economies, which are each quite small individually, face quite strong constraints on their conduct of monetary policy, independently of whether they participate in a single European currency. But monetary policy undoubtedly would be more constrained within EMU. Whether this should be seen as a disadvantage or benefit depends on one's confidence in the national monetary authorities to use monetary independence wisely. This is an area of policy in which a government has a great capacity to get it wrong. The point has wide application: modern governments retain great powers, but in a modern interdependent world, many of these powers are negative ones to mess things up, not positive ones to direct events for the good.

Table 2.1
Growth and volatility of G7 economies, 1970-93

	Increase in GDP (% per year)	Standard deviation of growth rate	No of years of declining GDP
Japan	4.0	2.0	1
Canada	3.3	2.5	2
Italy	2.7	2.3	2
France	2.5	1.6	1
USA	2.5	2.2	5
West Germany	2.3	2.1	3
UK	1.9	2.5	6

Source: OECD. *National Accounts/Main Economic Indicators.*

Domestic economic policy: what will be left?

What, then, will EMU imply for the conduct of economic policy? First and foremost it implies a single exchange-rate and monetary policy. With EMU, participating countries will give up their power to set monetary policy independently. National central banks will become branch offices of the ECB, which will set a common monetary policy across the EMU. The only relevant exchange rate will be that of the common currency, the euro, against the currencies of countries outside the EMU zone.

Despite the common monetary policy, there will remain some differences in interest rates reflecting differences in the markets' perception of the riskiness of the asset. But there will be no ability for national governments to manipulate this difference for reasons of macroeconomic performance.

Fiscal freedom?

In the absence of independent monetary policy, what scope will there be for an independent fiscal policy? In principle, a monetary union need place no constraints on the scope for an independent national fiscal policy. National governments could be free to borrow as they choose, either in euro markets or elsewhere. However, a major concern is that profligate countries will find it easier to run up debt, with the risk that more responsible countries will be left to pick up the bill. These concerns have led to the requirement of "no bail-out": the ECB is clearly prevented by the Maastricht treaty from bailing out profligate countries by financing their public deficits.

Other responses have been the convergence criteria laid down in the Maastricht treaty and the stability pact, renamed and agreed to as the "stability and growth pact" at the Dublin summit in December 1996. The Maastricht treaty constrains excessive borrowing both in and ahead of EMU, while the stability pact proposes somewhat more stringent constraints. Both have the same objective of avoiding the destabilisation of EMU by irresponsible national fiscal policies.

However, constraints intended to stop irresponsible fiscal policy can also limit the scope for governments to engage in prudent stabilising fiscal policies. The Maastricht treaty and stability pact can be interpreted as limiting the ability of individual countries to allow fiscal policy to operate in a stabilising way over the business cycle through the operation of so-called fiscal stabilisers. Critics of this aspect of EMU see it leading to an unnecessarily bumpy macroeconomic performance. We discuss this and related points in more detail in Chapter 4. On whatever interpretation, it seems likely that national fiscal policy will be constrained in EMU. But, if well thought out, such constraints may be helpful. Much will depend in practice on the effectiveness of the fiscal oversight carried out by the Council of Ministers and the ECB.

Competing over taxes

A final concern over fiscal policy is whether EMU will bring with it greater constraints on the ability of national governments to choose tax policy independently. This could involve EMU-wide constraints on tax rates, the definition of tax bases, and other details of tax policy. However, this does not enter the Maastricht treaty, and it is not clear why it should follow from EMU. Growing goods and labour market integration does place some limits on the freedom of individual national governments to set taxes as they choose, because high taxes may lead to some movement of production, sales or people to other, lower tax jurisdictions.

These constraints may be seen at work in the USA, where individual states set their own sales and income taxes, but have to do so with an eye on the possibility of people moving away to other more tax-favourable states. This does not prevent a fair degree of interstate variation in tax rates. But in the European context, these constraints arise anyway from growing integration as a consequence of the single European market. EMU will not add to these constraints unless the single currency brings greater integration in Europe. But such greater integration, which advocates of EMU see as a possibility, would be a major benefit of a single currency, not offset by any resulting tightening of tax policy constraints. Equally, non-participation in EMU would remove constraints on the setting of tax policy only if less market integration followed from non-participation, and this would represent a major cost of non-EMU.

The upshot is that within EMU governments will lose the capacity to use, or abuse, monetary policy and may face tighter limits on borrowing and deficits, but will otherwise retain powers over tax and spending decisions. There will be continued scope for choosing the government spending/tax level, even if decisions over the deficit are more constrained. But with less emphasis on the traditional tools of macroeconomic policy, it is likely that EMU will accentuate the trend, already instigated by globalisation of capital and other markets, towards greater emphasis on national management by microeconomic policy.

Creeping federalism?

Frequently juxtaposed with the diminishing powers of national governments is the concern that EMU will bring with it a major shift of powers to the European level. The double F-word appears: *fear of federation.* To those nationalists of whatever country for whom the nation-state is sacrosanct, this is potentially the most powerful argument against EMU. But even for pragmatists who are prepared to see a transfer of powers to Brussels if that is effective, there is concern about an over-centralised, unresponsive and bureaucratic Europe. We pick this argument up more fully in Chapter 4; here we provide an historical context for the debate.

Historical examples

Some historical lessons can be drawn from the experience of regions that have successfully moved to a single currency in the past century or so. There are several primary examples, all drawn from a similar epoch.

- Germany, which came together in political and economic union in the 1860s under the leadership of Bismarck.
- Italy, which came together in a political union in 1860, and moved to a single currency in 1862 when a royal decree made the lira legal tender.
- The USA, which forged its federation from the Civil War.
- Switzerland, whose separate cantons came together progressively from the 1850s onwards, adopting a common currency in 1870.
- The German-Austrian Monetary Union, which lasted a decade from 1857.
- The Latin Monetary Union, which lasted from 1865 for just over 60 years, but is long forgotten.
- The Scandinavian Monetary Union from 1872 until 1931.

German monetary unification: customs union preceded political union and monetary union

1815: Congress of Vienna: left 35 principalities and four free cities with full sovereignty over coinage and money systems (and weights and measures). Multiple (silver and gold) coinages coexisted, and paper money.
1834: Creation of free-trade Zollverein, removing internal customs barriers, excluding Austria.
1837: Munich coinage treaty, agreed by states south of the Main: specified coinage standards, leading to Zollverein-wide Dresden coinage convention of 1838, establishing fixed exchange rates between the two currency areas of the Zollverein.
1854: Trade treaty with Austria.
1857: Vienna coinage treaty linked Austria to Zollverein coinage systems, which were rationalised; forbade inconvertible paper money.
1871: Political union: creation of Reich (excluding Austria) with multiple coinages. Wilhelm takes title of Kaiser after Julius Caesar.
1876: Monetary unification with creation of Reichsbank followed two coinage acts (1871 and 1873), which limited the freedom of states to issue coins.

Lessons to be gleaned

A feature common to all these cases is that monetary union took place in the context of the gold standard, which gave rather little autonomy to national governments anyway; this now contrasts with the European countries that in joining EMU will be giving up powers of independent monetary policy. Despite this important difference, some lessons can be gleaned from the differing experiences of these countries in moving to monetary union.

• In monetary unions where political integration did not ensue (the Latin Monetary Union, the German-Austrian Monetary Union and the Scandinavian Monetary Union), monetary union did not last.

• Monetary union operated for a very considerable period without significant fiscal transfers through a central federal budget. This is not very surprising, since governments in the 19th and well into the 20th century were very small, and taxes were low. This gives support to those who argue that EMU can operate without significant fiscal transfers between member states; we pick up this point in Chapter 4 and consider whether it has continued validity in the different political, economic and social conditions of the late 20th century.

• The countries varied enormously in the extent to which political union preceded or followed monetary union. In the case of the USA, as we have noted, political union came first, and the national currency was introduced swiftly by the victorious North as a potent symbol of the new political federation. In Germany, too, Prussian might was the primary force for integration, and economic and monetary union followed behind. But in Italy, the political forces for integration were weak (a fact that persists to the present day), and economic and monetary union ran ahead of political union. In Switzerland, the political forces at the centre of the federation were weak at the outset, and have remained so: while the centre has gradually acquired more powers, major powers have remained with cantons, the second tier of Swiss government between the federal and the local (commune) level. This suggests two things: monetary union can precede political centralisation, and the degree of political centralisation needed in the long run can be quite limited.

• In some of these countries the move to monetary union was not at all smooth. Although the US federal reserve system works very smoothly and effectively today, its evolution was far from straightforward. For much of the 19th century, US banking lacked any form of central control or regulation, and bank failures were rife. The evolution of the federal reserve system to its present form took several decades, starting at the end of the 19th century, and was characterised by struggles for influence by the emerging reserve banks of the key states. In Italy, too, the move to an effective and efficient monetary union took time, requiring both the evolution of efficient techniques of monetary control and the resolution of conflicts between different parts of the union. It may well be that the modern EMU venture will experience similar transitional instabilities, though the detailed plans being worked out from the Maastricht blueprint by the European Monetary Institute (EMI), the precursor of the ECB, may avoid the worst of these.

The US road to monetary union

Pre-1865: Before the Civil War, state banks organised under different laws for each state, each issuing its own bank notes.
1861-65 Civil War: Confederate currency eliminated.
1863-65: National banking acts passed, aimed at eliminating pre-Civil War problems and raising revenue to fund war; but no federal central bank. Tax on notes issued by state banks unless authorised by federal government.
1873, 1884, 1890, 1893, 1907: Major panics in national banking.
1908: In response to 1907 panic, creation of the national monetary commission to study US monetary system, and emergency powers to groups of banks.
1913-14: Passing of Federal Reserve Act and start of its operation.
1914-30: Tensions in relations between Fed and state banks.

Also relevant to the debate over European federalism is the history to date of the EU itself. It is important to note that the EU has already seen a progressive strengthening of the powers of the centre relative to the member states. This has happened first through the original Rome treaty, signed by the founding members in 1957; then with the single European act of 1986; and most recently with the Maastricht treaty of 1992. The expansion of these powers is summarised in Appendix 1.

Europe is a federation already

The EU has already demonstrated a significant trend towards a loose form of federation (or confederation). It is important to note that many of the additional powers passed to the federal level in the Maastricht treaty have little to do with EMU: they have to do with additional powers of the European Parliament, increased areas to which qualified majority voting applies, and new policy areas such as foreign affairs. The UK's opt-out from EMU and the social chapter limit the extension of federal powers somewhat, but nonetheless Maastricht still brings with it a significant extension of federal powers in Europe.

The crucial point is that the EU is already a federation, albeit a loose one. It is appropriate for those who argue that the UK should leave the EU to use the F-word and inveigh against the evils of European federalism. For others, the relevant debate concerns the form of federation that they want, not whether they want one. A strict application of the principle of subsidiarity (taking decisions at the lowest appropriate level) would imply that Brussels and the centre gets involved in only those areas of policy that can only be effectively handled at the centre, and would let go of other areas. This could be a slim, decentralised federation, along Swiss lines. Or Europe could go in a highly centralised direction, moving closer to the model offered by nation states such as the UK and France. This is a political choice for Europe: even with EMU, the Swiss example demonstrates the point that, if constituent cultures prefer it, a federation need not be highly centralised. Some, particularly Eurosceptics, may see the choice as pre-empted, arguing that the EU is set inexorably in a centralising direction. But this in not inevitable, particularly if EMU triggers a wider political debate on the future direction of Europe.

It is not helpful to the debate on EMU, and indeed on the EU more generally, to use the term "federal" as an absolute, and not a relative, term. The EU is already a loose federation. The choice for Europe is not between a federation and a non-federation, but rather the appropriate degree of federalism. The nations of the EU face a choice between a very loose federation (or confederation) and a much tighter, more centralised union. For the foreseeable future, the only realistic possibility is some adjustment of the loose confederation that is already in place; in the longer term, it seems equally conceivable that this embryonic federation will either grow into a tighter, more cohesive federation or unravel in acrimony and discord.

Chapter 3 The path to EMU

Proto-EMU

Developments since 1970

Economic and monetary union has long been an aspiration of the European Community. As long ago as 1970, only 13 years after the Rome treaty was signed by the six original members of the European Economic Community (France, Germany, Italy and Benelux), the Werner plan proposed a decade-long transition to a single currency by 1980. At that time the Bretton Woods system of fixed exchange rates, which pegged the currencies of the major industrial countries to the dollar, was still in place. The relative fixity of exchange rates gave plausibility to the plan for a single currency within the Community. But the proposal came at the tail-end of the Bretton Woods era, at a time when rising worldwide inflation and the greatly increasing mobility of international capital were making it increasingly difficult for governments to maintain fixed parities.

EU milestones

1958: European Economic Community established, including Belgium, France, Italy, Luxembourg, Netherlands, West Germany.
1962: European Commission first proposes monetary union.
1960s: UK applies for membership of European Communities and is rejected.
1970: Werner plan for European monetary union.
1972: "Snake" exchange-rate mechanism set up as Bretton Woods system breaks down.
1973: Denmark, Ireland and UK join EEC.
1979: European monetary system (EMS) founded, including exchange-rate mechanism (ERM).
1981: Greece joins EEC.
1986: Single European Act (SEA) lays foundation for single market. Portugal and Spain join Community.
1991: Maastricht treaty agreed, leading to establishment of EU and setting out plans for EMU.
1994: European Monetary Institute established.
1995: Austria, Finland and Sweden join EU.

Within two years of the publication of the Werner plan, the Bretton Woods system collapsed. Exchange rates started to fluctuate markedly against each other. The EC attempted to create a zone of fixed intra-European parities, leaving each currency free to float against outside currencies such as the dollar and yen. This European currency "snake" was a precursor of the European

Figure 3.1
Consumer-price inflation, 1954-80

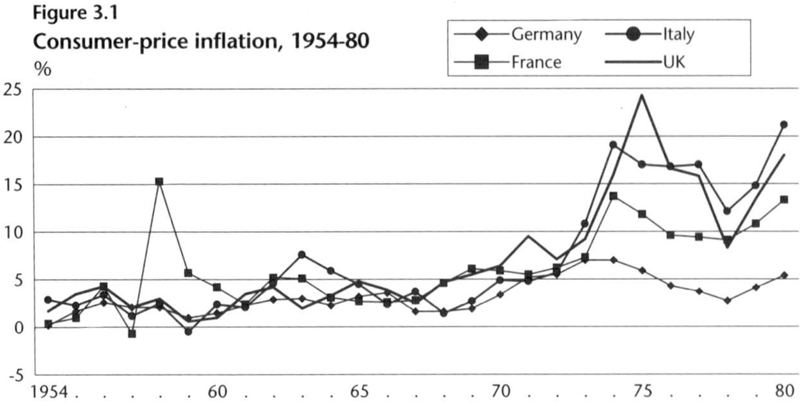

Source: IMF, *International Financial Statistics*.

Figure 3.2
Exchange rates, 1952-80
Inverted scales

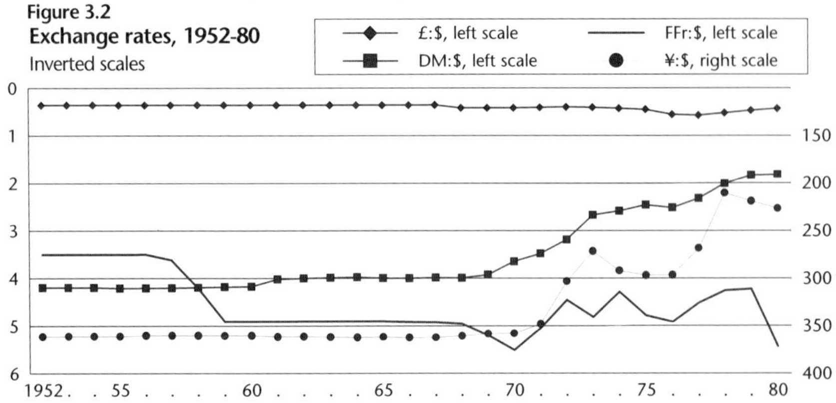

Source: IMF, *International Financial Statistics*.

Monetary System (EMS) that followed in 1979. But it quickly failed. Thoughts of monetary union were set aside as inflation took off in the industrial countries following the Organisation of Petroleum Exporting Countries' decision to raise the price of oil in 1973-74. The resulting differences in inflation among European countries made plans for monetary union implausible.

The search for exchange-rate stability

In 1979, after nearly a decade of exchange-rate turbulence, the Community launched the European Monetary System (EMS). This was intended to make Europe a zone of exchange-rate stability. A decade later, the EMS was regarded as a proven success, and many judged that the time was ripe to develop the system further. Jacques Delors, then president of the European Commission, produced the Delors report, proposing once more that the EC move in stages to monetary union. The project was enshrined in the Maastricht treaty at the end of 1991.

When the EMS fell apart during the foreign-exchange crises of September 1992 and July 1993, it seemed that history was repeating itself, and that the objective of EMU had once again fallen victim to financial-market speculation and exchange-rate instability. Those opposed to the idea of a single European currency and all that it entails expressed relief. They argued that Europe, now spared the distraction of creating a single currency, would make faster progress towards creating a truly pan-European single market, through trade integration with the newly liberated countries of eastern Europe.

Key features of the EMS

European monetary system

- Established in 1979.

- All EEC countries became members but UK did not join exchange-rate mechanism (ERM) until 1990.

- Objectives:
  - Exchange-rate stability.
  - Helping to control inflation (D-mark anchor).
  - Economic policy cooperation.

- Led to creation of a new "basket" currency, the ecu.

- Main feature is the ERM:
  - Currencies to fluctuate in band plus or minus 2.25% of central ecu rate.
  - Wider band allowed for some countries (Italy, Spain, UK).
  - Currency peg maintained by intervention, interest rate changes and capital controls (until mid-1980s).
  - Realignments permitted by mutual agreement.

- 1992-93 crisis led UK and Italy to depart and bands to be widened to plus or minus 15%.

This view of the significance of the 1992-93 EMS crisis has yet to be justified by events. EMU is not yet derailed. It still seems probable, for better or worse, that a significant group of EU members will proceed to create a single currency—though exactly how probable, when it will happen, and how large the group will be are all far from clear.

In the following pages, we describe the background. We consider the significance and causes of the EMS crisis; why, in its aftermath, it is still possible for European countries to consider moving to a single currency; and the importance of some of the technical issues involved in this transition. We will make, for the moment, no attempt to discuss the merits or otherwise of the move to a single currency. That will be a matter for subsequent chapters. Our concern here is to set the historical and technical scene for the analysis that follows.

The EMS crisis: causes and significance

In September 1992 a wave of speculative pressures engulfed the EMS. Starting with the Finnish markka, which was attempting to shadow the D-mark from outside the EMS, it moved on to the Italian lira, the Spanish peseta and then sterling. Despite the best efforts of the authorities, the peseta was forced to devalue by 5% within the system, and the lira and pound to withdraw from it.

Despite acute pressures on the French franc, its parity was sustained with much help from the Bundesbank.

Less than a year later, in July 1993, a further wave of speculation engulfed the system. The authorities were forced to widen the normal, accepted band of currency variation from plus or minus 2.25% of the central rate to plus or minus 15%. With such wide margins of variation, the revised EMS provides very little constraint on currency movements. The proposal of the Delors report, that a progressive tightening of the EMS provide a gradual glide-path for currencies down to EMU, had been fatally undermined.

The debacle from nowhere

The EMS crisis of September 1992 appeared from nowhere. Despite the claims of many to have predicted it, there is little evidence that markets were anticipating it even a few weeks before. Until the crisis, the system had enjoyed a period of remarkable stability. In its early years, frequent and sometimes large realignments of its participating currencies were required to hold the system together, but by 1992 some five and a half years had elapsed since the last general realignment. In other words, the system appeared to have evolved from its soft form of earlier years into a hard EMS, in which currency parities did not change. To many, this showed that the system's members were ready for the move to full monetary union.

Figure 3.3
D-mark exchange rates
3 Qtr 1996=100

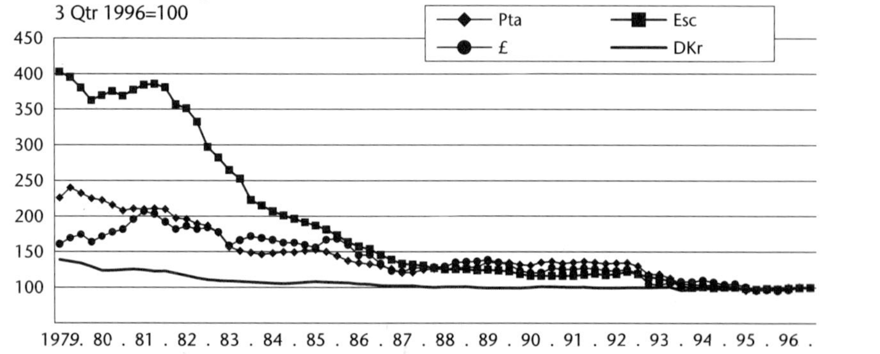

Source: Datastream.

Figure 3.4
D-mark exchange rates
3 Qtr 1996=100

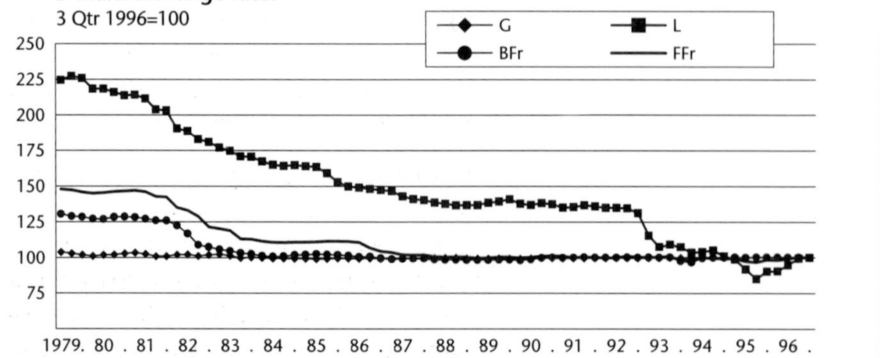

Source: Datastream.

Figure 3.5
Long-term government bond differentials, 1987 to September 1992
%; national bond minus German long bond

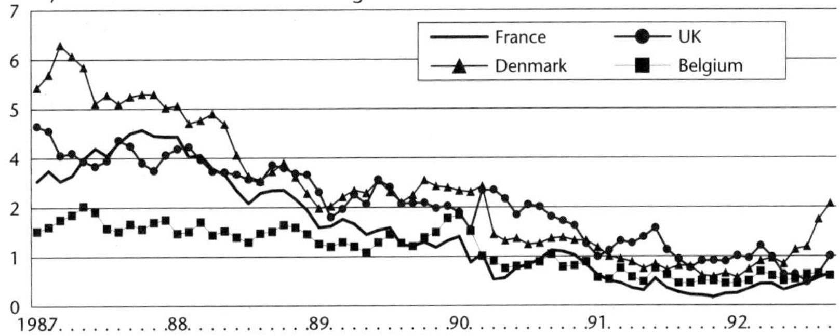

Source: Datastream.

Figure 3.6
Long-term government bond differentials, 1987 to September 1992
%; national bond minus German long bond

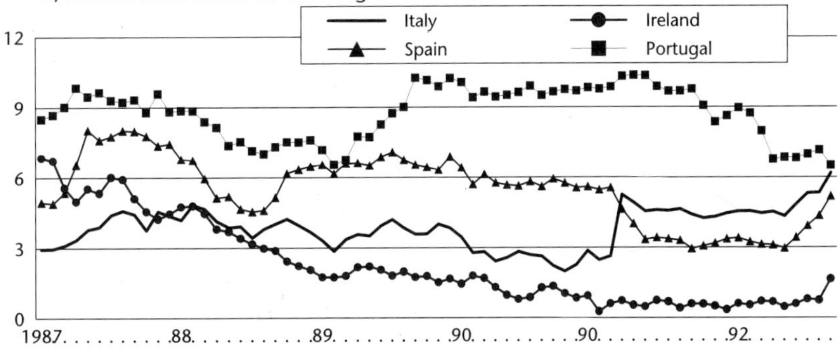

Source: Datatsream.

Narrower differentials and growing confidence

Between 1987 and 1992 there had in fact been one partial realignment of the system: the lira's parity was adjusted on January 1, 1990. But because of the way it was carried out, this had served only to reinforce confidence. It had been a model technical realignment of the central parity, keeping the floor for the lira unchanged as Italy moved from the special wide band that it had enjoyed hitherto to the normal narrow band. It was therefore seen as a strengthening, not a weakening, of the hard EMS. In the period up to September 1992, the differentials between German and non-German long-bond yields narrowed significantly (with the exception of Italy), demonstrating the growing confidence of the foreign-exchange markets in the maintenance of the existing currency parities and the possible merging of national moneys, as proposed by Mr Delors, into a single currency.

However, once foreign exchange markets lost confidence, the hard EMS was bound to shatter. Even in ordinary circumstances, the volume of forex transactions, relative to the resources at the disposal of central banks and national treasuries, is vast. At times of crisis, the tide is such that the authorities cannot hope to hold it back. In 1992, the average daily level of transactions in foreign exchange markets was estimated to be in excess of $1 trillion—more than the value of the UK's total annual output. And this was only half the story: another

$1 trillion, equivalent to another year's worth of the UK's GDP, was traded each day in the forward and futures markets. Given such volumes, the authorities have very little room for manoeuvre if a general market view emerges that a currency is overvalued. The resulting flood of money is just too great to withstand. This is what the British treasury experienced on the Wednesday (Black or White, according to taste) when sterling was forced out of the EMS by a gigantic surge of one-way speculative pressure.

Why did it happen?

What were the factors that led the markets to a successful attack on the system's parities? It is possible, more easily with the benefit of hindsight, to identify a variety of contributing factors. Several countries—notably the UK and Italy, but also Spain and Portugal—had failed to make the fundamental adjustment to Germany's earlier record of low inflation. As a result, their EMS parities were vulnerable.

The UK had experienced inflation at a higher-than-German rate since joining the system two years before. It had therefore experienced a significant loss of competitiveness, and this came on top of joining at a parity (of DM2.95) already judged by many commentators to have been over-ambitious. Even though Italy's headline rate of inflation had converged towards Germany's, inflation in unit labour costs had not converged to the same degree, so that Italy's manufacturing sector had also been losing competitiveness steadily since the last major realignment in 1987.

Germany, having to contend with rising inflationary pressures after unification, was out of kilter with Europe's other economies. Other countries, including France, Italy and the UK, were struggling with recession and rising unemployment. As the Bundesbank drove up interest rates to contain German inflation, so other European central banks were forced to raise their interest rates to maintain their EMS parities, even though this worsened recession at home. Unsurprisingly, the foreign exchange markets asked how long the French, Italian, Spanish and UK governments would be able to sustain these high interest rates, unpopular with the electorate. The UK was particularly singled out because of the political importance of the floating interest rates charged on its ubiquitous mortgages. The relatively low level of the dollar, which boosted US penetration of European markets, added to the recessionary pressures.

Uncertainties over ratification of the Maastricht treaty added to the resulting speculation. Monetary union required the treaty to be ratified unanimously by all countries; a single veto would have scuppered the treaty and hence the prospect of EMU. Several European countries, particularly France and Italy, were holding on to their EMS parities with a view to participation in EMU. If the Maastricht treaty was not ratified, then they would have less reason to struggle to maintain their parity. Any faltering in the ratification process therefore constituted a good reason for hedging exchange-rate exposure, thereby putting further pressure on the currency.

In practice, there were many such hesitations. In their referendum of June 1992, the Danish electorate voted against Maastricht, a vote that was reversed only after a year's delay. In late August and early September 1992, it became clear that the French referendum on Maastricht would be a close thing. These political uncertainties fuelled more speculation in the foreign exchange market. Tactical errors by, and divisions among, the principal central banks and authorities responsible for maintaining the system's exchange-rate mechanism added to the problems.

Deeper causes

These factors were the proximate causes of the collapse of the EMS. But the system was vulnerable for more fundamental reasons as well. A fixed exchange-rate system places heavy obligations on the authorities of the country at the core of the system. The Bretton Woods system worked quite well as long as the USA adopted cautious macroeconomic policies; once it moved to deficit financing and a looser monetary policy in the 1960s, the consequent rising inflationary pressures worldwide led to the weakening and eventual collapse of the fixed exchange-rate system. In simple terms, Bretton Woods collapsed because the USA exported inflation which its partners did not want.

The EMS collapsed for the opposite reason: Germany exported recession. This was not immediate, because the first phase of German unification was a booming German economy and booming exports by other European countries to Germany. But the later phase saw high German interest rates to curb German inflation, and falling German demand. Lower export sales to Germany, coupled with a need to match high German interest rates to maintain EMS parities, led to recession in other European countries.

Arguably, sustaining any hard (ie, infrequently adjusted) EMS requires the Bundesbank not merely to sail on in the expectation that the flotilla will follow, but to take account of cyclical developments elsewhere in Europe, not just in Germany. Otherwise membership of the system may prove too onerous, and other member states will come under pressure to devalue. Once the markets perceive this risk to be increasing, speculation may follow: a vicious circle begins to operate, leading ultimately to a forced devaluation.

To preserve a form of hard EMS, the Bundesbank needed to behave more like a central bank of Europe and less like the central bank of Germany. It is no criticism of the Bundesbank to point out that it failed to do this: taking account of developments in Europe as a whole would have contravened its constitutional obligation to be concerned with price stability in Germany. But this dilemma does give weight to the view, expressed by the UK's prime minister, John Major, after the crisis in September 1992, that "faultlines" in the EMS contributed to what happened.

At an even deeper level, it is arguable that quasi-fixed exchange-rate systems, such as Bretton Woods and the EMS, are by their very nature hopelessly vulnerable to speculative attack. Maintaining such a system in the face of today's potentially massive capital flows requires a high degree of coordination among the participating central banks. Inevitably, however, there are limits to the degree of cooperation that is feasible among independent monetary authorities, each with its own domestic pressures (economic and political) to contend with. Economic shocks and other difficulties of the kind discussed above expose these limits, which the foreign exchange markets can then cruelly exploit. The chief lesson of the EMS crisis of 1992-93 is that fixed exchange rates are sustainable only if monetary sovereignty is pooled—and the purest form of pooling is to create a single money-issuing authority. It is important to analyse this episode properly in order to draw the correct lessons from it. Two points are crucial.

Lesson 1: The failure of the EMS does not seal EMU's fate

The first is that it is wrong to infer, as some do, that EMU must suffer the same fate as the EMS. The two differ fundamentally, in that a monetary union requires the pooling of monetary sovereignty, not monetary cooperation, the limits of which were the root problem of the EMS. Given pooled monetary policy, the EMU could not be subject to foreign exchange speculation of the kind that brought down the EMS, any more than could the sterling value of the Scottish pound.

This helps to explain why EMU is still on the agenda, despite the EMS crisis. Indeed, one objective of proponents of EMU is precisely to create a European Central Bank that can set an EMU-wide monetary policy that takes account of economic developments in the EMU bloc as a whole, not just in Germany as the Bundesbank did. This is not to argue that EMU will be free from other sorts of pressures, or that the *transition* to EMU will be free of speculative problems: it can be argued that it will be harder for the ECB to establish credibility under these conditions. We return to this question later in the report.

Lesson 2: Restoring a narrow-band EMS may be impossible

The second conclusion is that it is bound to be extremely difficult, and perhaps impossible, to restore any sort of hard, or narrow-band, EMS. This is highly relevant to EMU, since an important debate is in progress about the future relationship between the euro and the currencies of the EU's member states not participating in EMU. One proposal was to restore a narrow-band EMS to peg these outsider currencies to the euro. But at the EU summit in Dublin in 1996 it was agreed that the exchange rates of the "outs" would be allowed to fluctuate by up to 15% either side of their euro parity, although some could opt to negotiate narrower bands. Participation in the system would be voluntary.

Narrow bands are feasible for countries that have achieved a very high degree of nominal convergence, such as the Benelux vis-à-vis Germany. But they are much more difficult to sustain for the "pre-ins", which have, by definition, failed to achieve the required convergence to participate in EMU. We return to this point in a later chapter, but the lesson from this brief history is that a narrow-band EMS for the "outs" would probably not be viable.

The transition to EMU

The Maastricht treaty laid down both a path and criteria for the transition to a single European currency. The Delors report in 1989 had envisaged a three-stage transition to EMU. In the first stage, countries were to join the EMS, complete the single market programme, and enhance their mutual macroeconomic cooperation. In the second stage, the European Monetary Institute (EMI) would be created to oversee the preparation for EMU, replacing the committee of central bank governors as the formal mechanism for cooperation on monetary policy in the EU. In the third stage, the currencies of the countries participating would be fixed irrevocably (they would become, in effect, different versions of one money), a central bank would be created to control the common monetary policy of the participating countries, and eventually national currencies would be replaced by the single European currency.

From EMS to EMU: the Delors report of 1989

Stage 1
- All countries join EMS.
- Completion of single market.
- Closer economic cooperation.
- Strengthening of competition policies.

Stage 2
- EMI replaces committee of EU central bank governors.

Stage 3
- To begin January 1, 1997 but not later than January 1, 1999.
- Participants satisfy convergence criteria.
- Irrevocably fixed exchange rates (no bands).
- ECB with full power to control EU monetary policy.
- Euro to replace national currencies "in due course".
- ECB independent but EU Council of finance ministers (Ecofin) to decide exchange-rate policy. Could lead to conflict.
- EU to limit budget deficits.

Unchangeable

The Maastricht plan

This staged process was incorporated largely intact into the Maastricht treaty, signed in December 1991 and ratified in the following two years. The treaty set out a timetable for the transition to EMU and laid down requirements and conditions on the countries participating. Under the terms of the treaty, the EMI came into being in January 1994. Stage 3 could have begun at the earliest in January 1997, if a majority of member states qualified for participation (which did not happen) but not later than January 1999, even if only a minority of countries qualified.

However, the drafting of the treaty allowed for the Council of Ministers to specify *before* the second deadline a *later* starting date. The Council decided in Madrid in December 1995 that January 1, 1999 *would* be the start date. But if there is a need to delay the start of EMU to allow more time for countries to prepare, or if a general wish emerges to defer EMU indefinitely, then practical politics mean that this decision could be revisited; and the possibility in the treaty of a later start date would make that reconsideration easier.

With the start of EMU, the ECB will be created, replacing the EMI. (In practice, the EMI will become the ECB.) The ECB will have full powers to control monetary policy within the EMU zone. The national central banks of the participating countries will become, in effect, branch offices of the ECB, in the way that the regional reserve banks in the USA act as branches of the federal reserve.

The Maastricht treaty laid down only the broad outlines of the transition to EMU, leaving the details to be worked out by the European Commission, the EMI (and later the ECB), and the Council of Ministers. Subsequent discussion and negotiation have fleshed out the transitional arrangements and timetable.

The current working assumption is that, the earlier starting date for EMU having been missed, in the first half of 1998 the decision will be made as to which member states will participate in EMU. The monetary union will then start on January 1, 1999 with the locking together of the currencies of the participating countries, and the euro, the single European currency, will come into being, at least for wholesale money-market transactions. It is then envisaged that in a short period three years later (in the first few weeks or months of 2002) euro notes and coins will be issued on a large scale to replace national currencies, which will gradually be withdrawn. From that point on, EMU will operate with the euro in all forms of financial transactions.

From here to the euro

In more detail, what is envisaged is a three-phase transition. In the first or launch phase in 1998, agreement would be reached on the participating countries, and the precise timing of the start of EMU and the introduction of the euro would be settled (it is likely to be January 1, 1999, though this timetable might slip). Final preparations would then begin: any remaining legal issues would be resolved, arrangements for producing the new notes and coins would be made, and the countdown for the banking and financial community to switch from national currencies to the euro would start.

The second phase of about three years (from 1999 until the start of 2002) would see the locking of exchange rates and the introduction of the euro as a currency in its own right (as opposed to the European currency unit (ecu), which is a basket of currencies). The ECB would take responsibility for monetary policy within the euro area, and would conduct monetary and exchange-rate policy in terms of the euro, not national currencies.

This phase would see the introduction of euro markets for money, interbank, capital and foreign exchange transactions, as well as a system for wholesale euro interbank settlements. All new national government debt would be denominated in euros. Banks and financial institutions would continue to transfer their operations from national currencies to the euro, but private agents would be free to continue to contract in national currencies if they wished.

The third phase, lasting several weeks or months, depending on feasibility, would see the withdrawal of national currencies and their replacement by the euro. All contracts would be converted from national currencies to euros, without renegotiation of other terms of the contract. (This may be far from plain sailing for ecu contracts, as we will discuss later.) At this point, the single currency would at last be an established fact.

Making the grade: the convergence criteria

Countries wishing to participate in EMU must satisfy certain convergence criteria. Two of these criteria relate to nominal convergence, two to fiscal convergence. The criteria for nominal convergence are that a country must have an inflation rate within 1.5% (for the past two years) of the average inflation rate of the three countries with the lowest inflation rates; and a long bond yield within 2% of the average long bond yields of the same three countries. The fiscal criteria require the country to have a public deficit ratio no more than 3% of GDP, and a level of debt no more than 60% of GDP.

The transition in detail

The Commission's Green Paper on EMU proposes that Stage 3 of the transition to EMU should itself fall into three phases, occupying the next five or so years.

Phase 3A: Launch of EMU, maximum duration one year (1998)
Start of the phase:
- List of participating member states.
- Date of start of EMU announced.
- Date of final changeover to the single currency.

Throughout the phase:
- Stepping-up of preparations and implementation of measures that will, if possible, have been adopted beforehand.
- Production of notes and coins.
- Legal framework.
- National steering structure.
- Banking and financial community changeover plan.

Phase 3B: Start of EMU, maximum duration three years (1999-2001)
- The start of EMU with irrevocably locked exchange rates.

Start of the phase:
- Fixing of conversion rates.
- Euro becomes a currency in its own right.
- Monetary and exchange-rate policy interventions in euro.
- Interbank, capital, monetary and exchange markets in euro.
- New government debt issued in euro.
- Wholesale payment systems in euro.

Throughout the phase:
- Banks and financial institutions continue the changeover.
- Public and private operators other than banks proceed with the switch to the euro as and when they wish.

Phase 3C: Introduction of the euro, several weeks duration (2002)
- Completion of EMU when only euro is legal tender, and national currencies are withdrawn.
- Euro notes and coins introduced.
- Banks will have completed the changeover of retail business payment systems.
- Notes and coins denominated in national currency are withdrawn.
- Only the euro circulates.
- Public and private operators complete the switch to the euro.

Who will qualify?

An economic forecast of which countries might meet these criteria in 1997 is provided in Appendix 2. The inflation and long-bond criteria are tightly specified. By contrast, the fiscal criteria provide a variety of escape clauses. Loosely interpreted, these say that countries may be deemed to satisfy the criteria if the indicators are merely close to the targets, or (even less demanding) if they are moving firmly in the right direction. This leaves plenty of scope for disagreement. Up to now, Germany has preferred to interpret the criteria strictly (even though it will itself struggle to hit the budget-deficit target in 1997), whereas other member states incline to a laxer view.

Four tests

The convergence criteria

- Inflation convergence: to qualify a country must have an inflation rate which is less than the average of the three lowest country inflation rates plus 1.5%.

- For a period of two years before EMU a country must have an average long-term nominal interest rate which does not exceed by more than 2% the average interest rate of the three countries with the lowest inflation rates.

- The government budgetary position: the government deficit to GDP ratio must be less than 3% and the stock of government debt to GDP ratio must be less than 60%. These may be waived if the ratio is heading towards satisfying the criteria or if the departure is only temporary.

- The exchange rate must have remained within its ERM bands for the previous two years and there must have been no realignment of the currency.

In cases where there is any doubt, assessment may also make reference to other convergence criteria: integration of markets, balance of payments, unit wage costs, compatibility between national legislation, etc.

Two other conditions apply to participation: the currency has to have been within its normal ERM band for two years without devaluation, and the central bank has to be independent of government direction in the conduct of monetary policy. The ERM condition led both Finland and Italy to enter the ERM late in 1996, so as not to be debarred from participation in the first wave of EMU. These conditions together might represent a potential obstacle to UK participation in the first wave, even if a change of government opened up this as a possibility.

According to the Maastricht treaty, powers over fiscal policy will remain at the national level, though governments will be expected to conduct their fiscal policy after EMU in accordance with the fiscal convergence criteria. The Council of Ministers (Ecofin) will oversee the conduct of fiscal policy, and have the power to fine governments that breach the fiscal criteria, but beyond that will have no powers to direct the national conduct of fiscal policy. This has led to worry, particularly in Germany, that future restraints on irresponsible fiscal policy will be inadequate, and that EMU will encourage rising government borrowing and debt, driving up real interest rates. It has also led to concern that Ecofin (on which both "in" and "out" members of the EU will be represented, and which will also expand along with EU enlargement) is not the appropriate body for the oversight of fiscal policy within the EMU zone.

Tougher still: the "stability and growth pact"

This fear motivated the suggestion of a "stability pact" by Theo Waigel, the German finance minister, who originally proposed that the EMU participants should restrict their fiscal deficits to 1% of GDP, on average. This, it is argued,

Figure 3.7
EU general government deficit, 1997 forecasts

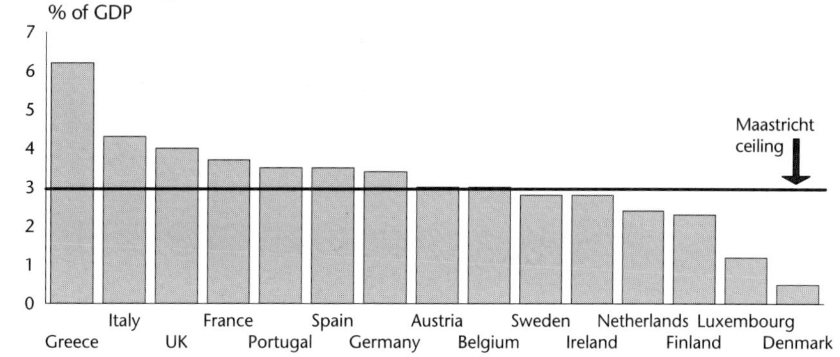

Source: EIU.

Figure 3.8
EU general government debt, 1997 forecasts

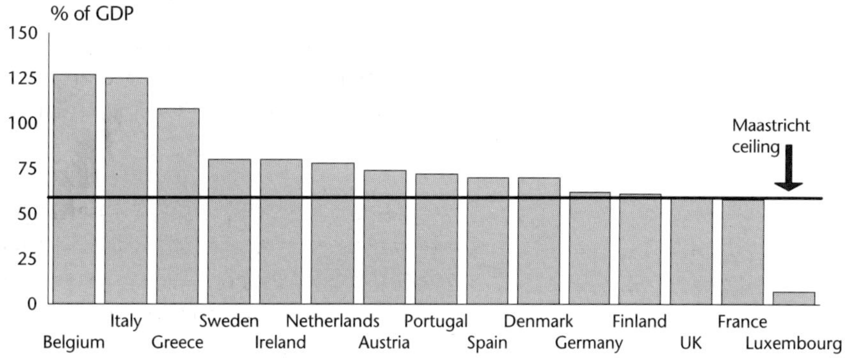

Source: EIU.

Figure 3.9
EU consumer-price inflation, 1997 forecasts

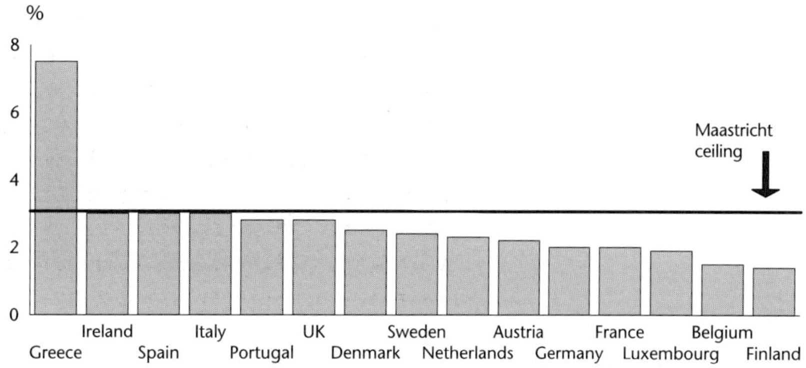

Source: EIU.

Figure 3.10
EU government bond yields, 1997 forecasts

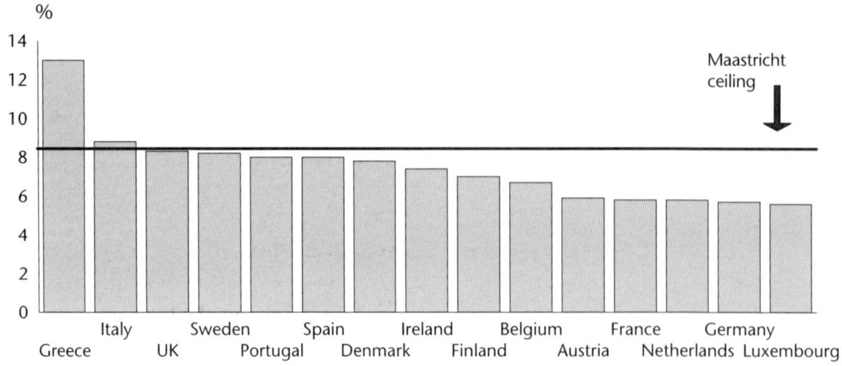

Source: EIU.

is needed to ensure that the Maastricht target of 3% is not breached during the course of the economic cycle. Automatic penalties for breaches of the 3% deficit ceiling were also proposed, with the suggestion that governments pay a deposit of 25% of any excess deficit over 3% of GDP. This would be forfeited if the excess deficit were not corrected in a specified time. Moreover, it was suggested that a "stability council" comprising EMU finance ministers (a subset of Ecofin) should oversee fiscal policy within EMU.

The Dublin summit of December 1996

These German proposals met with some opposition from other countries, notably France. But since it was clear that some form of stability pact was the necessary price of German participation, without which EMU was a non-starter, the Dublin summit in December 1996 agreed to the essentials of the German proposal, though under the face-saving name of the "stability and growth pact". This provides for fines of 0.2% of GDP for a breach of the 3% ceiling, with a further 0.1% for each further 1% breach of the ceiling, up to a maximum of 0.5% of GDP. The scale of these fines, while less than originally proposed, is substantial.

The German wish that such fines should be automatic was rejected, not least because it would have required a revision of the Maastricht Treaty which was impossible to contemplate. The procedure laid down in the Treaty is that, in the event of a breach of the 3% limit, the Commission will report to Ecofin, having considered whether there are exceptional circumstances that warrant the breach. Ecofin will then decide by a qualified majority whether an excessive deficit exists. The Dublin summit augmented this by agreeing that exemption from fines will be automatic in event of a natural disaster or if the country experiences a fall in GDP of 2% or more over a year. If the country has experienced a fall in the range 0.75-2%, Ecofin will have discretion in the levying of fines. With a fall smaller than 0.75%, the implication is that fines will be levied, though this will require the agreement of the ministers in Ecofin.

The result is a halfway house on fiscal policy: it seems that budget policy will be neither fully coordinated nor fully independent. This prompts several questions. Will the lack of a fully coordinated fiscal policy render EMU unworkable? Will the powers to fine provide a sufficient deterrent to irresponsible national fiscal policies, and if not, will that destabilise the monetary union? Or, on the contrary, will this constrained approach to fiscal policy prove unduly contractionary, both ahead of and in EMU, worsening the problem of European unemployment and slow growth? How will the ECB choose the nationality of the debt in which to conduct its open-market operations? How will this choice affect the conduct of fiscal policy? We return to these questions in Chapter 4, which discusses the macroeconomic implications of monetary union.

Problems ahead

Critics of EMU argue that, quite apart their other worries, the next stage in this gradual process of European monetary integration will be even more fraught than its predecessors. Indeed, many advocates of EMU are concerned on this score as well. Regardless of whether monetary union, once established, will be a success, getting there does pose problems in its own right. In principle, at least, these problems could be so severe that they might tip the balance against attempting to build EMU, even if the finished institution were deemed in itself to be a good thing. So the transitional difficulties warrant careful attention. We concentrate on three: confusion over the means of payment in the phase after the locking together of member currencies, when the euro and national currencies coexist; the possibility of speculation against the "irrevocably fixed" exchange rates of the euro during that same phase; and the contractionary effect of EU countries seeking to meet the Maastricht criteria ahead of 1997. Let us look at each of these transitional issues in turn.

Confusion: a many-headed euro?

Some EMU critics point out that the proposed transition to EMU contains the possibility of muddle in Phase 3B over the means of payment. In this phase the euro will have been introduced as a currency in its own right, and the banking system will start to convert to the use of euros. But national currencies will continue to be used in their home countries while acceptance of the euro in retail transactions will not be required. Will the euro be generally accepted in payment during this transitional phase, and if not won't its credibility suffer? Moreover, will prices for goods and services be quoted in both the national currency and the euro during this phase?

The problem of overlap should not be as intense as these queries imply. Phase 3B is expected to last three years: that is the time it will take to produce sufficient stocks of euro notes and coins. Until these are produced, euros will not circulate as notes and coins, and national notes and coins will provide the cash required for retail transactions. Only in Phase 3C, when the notes and coins are ready, will euro cash start to circulate, and then for only a short period (a matter of several weeks or perhaps two months) will they circulate alongside national currencies while the latter are phased out. There is therefore no prospect of an extended phase in which the euro could become ostracised. If the required euro notes and coins can be produced more quickly, there is the possibility that the date of the start of phase 3C will be advanced.

In phase 3B the euro will, however, be used for wholesale transactions in the banking system, and this will have consequences for the operation of banks in the transition, as we discuss in Chapter 6. It is also likely that other large payments, for example, in securities markets and between large companies, will be made increasingly in euros. The prevalence of this will depend partly on how quickly efficient electronic systems of euro payment are put in place, and this may vary across the participating countries.

It is also quite possible that euro payment by credit and debit cards will be introduced quickly, so that retail transactions could be effected electronically in euros. This prospect will depend upon the willingness of retailers to engage in dual pricing, which could prove costly in terms of extra labelling, training of staff, accounting records, etc. It may therefore make sense for retailers to delay euro pricing until just before the introduction of euro notes and coins in Phase 3C. This is a decision that individual retailers can be left to take on the basis of what the market demands.

It seems unlikely that the proposed process for the introduction of the euro will be chaotic. Reasonably planned, it can work as smoothly as did the UK's conversion to decimalisation in 1972. What is clear is that, as for that British conversion, the switch to the euro will be a big logistical operation, involving the replacement of the entire stock of national notes and coins by euros, a change in the unit of account by a very awkward and complicated decimal conversion, the conversion of all cash machines (ATMs, food and drink dispensers, etc), and the switch of accounts from national currencies to euros.

This will involve major costs, both in time and resources, and in terms of confusion over the new unit of account. For those who are sceptical of the benefits of EMU, these transitional costs are one more good reason for not proceeding. For those who see longer-term benefits from EMU, these one-off costs are not a good reason for holding back. The adoption of the euro may be a disorientating and disturbing process: not so disturbing as to swing the larger arguments for or against EMU one way or the other, but enough to raise doubts over whether the three-year, multi-currency interregnum will proceed as smoothly as currently planned.

Will speculation blow EMU apart?

Another transitional concern is that of speculation against the supposedly "irrevocably locked" exchange rates in the period leading up to 2002, when national currencies will continue to circulate against each other but at a fixed set of parities. The experience of the EMS in 1992-93 leads many to suspect that speculation will blow apart these fixed exchange rates and abort EMU before it has even started.

This concern is probably misplaced, though it could lead to an interesting test of the sincerity with which national governments and central banks (and the Bundesbank in particular) accept EMU as an irrevocable fact. As already noted, EMU's Phase 3B (1999-2001) will be quite different from the EMS. The ECB will have complete control over the conduct of monetary policy in the EMU zone, with full powers to instruct national central banks, whereas in the EMS, monetary control was divided among the participating central banks. Speculation against the prescribed exchange rates could succeed only if the ECB failed to do its job, and the new bank has every incentive to succeed in order to establish its reputation.

If speculation against the franc:D-mark rate, for example, builds up, the ECB need only expand the supply of D-marks and reduce the supply of francs, while retaining control of the overall money supply in the EMU zone. Its power to do this will match any market demand to exchange francs for D-marks that can be envisaged, but it could certainly require the Bundesbank to issue D-marks in a way that will make the return to the pre-EMU status quo impossible. Assuming that the national central banks will honour such obligations, the markets will quickly be convinced that there is nothing to be gained from speculating between different manifestations of the single currency, and the pressures will die away.

There is a much greater likelihood of currency speculation once the participating countries have been determined but before their exchange rates have been fixed, as the markets take positions on what the fixing rates will be. Severe currency instability ahead of EMU could be very damaging, weakening the credibility of particular currencies, and making life difficult (in both economic and political terms) within this or that participating economy on the very eve of EMU. One suggestion for reducing this danger of speculation ahead of the fixing of exchange rates is for the exchange rates to be announced in advance. If the markets believed those rates, and recognised the power of the ECB to make them stick, such a pre-announcement could help guide the markets in advance and avoid pre-fixing volatility. But if the markets thought that the authorities might revise the announced rates if market rates moved sufficiently far away, then announcing the rates in advance might increase speculation, not dampen it.

The ecu conundrum

There is also a technical problem in pre-announcing rates, arising from the decision, built into the Maastricht treaty, to convert the European currency unit (ecu), the existing European unit of account, into the euro on a one-to-one basis. The current ecu is a basket of currencies which includes both currencies that will participate in EMU (the "ins") and those that will not (the "outs"). What this means is that the final conversion rates of the participating currencies against the euro will imply an exchange rate of the euro against the average of the non-participating currencies—one that makes the ecu equal to one euro at the moment of conversion. Announcing these conversion rates in advance therefore implies a forecast of the exchange rate of the "in" currencies against the "out" currencies at that moment. If that forecast is wrong, as it almost certainly will be, then it will be impossible to fulfil the implied promises: the conversion rates of national currencies to the euro will be inconsistent with the one-to-one conversion of the ecu to the euro. The only feasible pre-announcement would be to announce the set of exchange rates among participating national currencies, and leave the market to determine the conversion rate of this block of currencies, and of the individual outsiders, into the euro as the market rates on the day of fixing. But to leave open the key conversion rate of national currencies into the future currency seems highly unsatisfactory.

For both the above reasons, therefore, it seems that the option of pre-announcement will not be followed. Similar difficulties may be associated with other forms of market guidance, such as the suggestion that locking should happen at rates that reflect the average of market rates over a given period.

Some instability of exchange rates before fixing therefore cannot be ruled out. It is unclear what the authorities will be able to do about this except attempt to ride it out. If the instability is great, then it could disrupt, and in extreme cases even derail, the transition to the single currency.

The third problem of transition is that of the macroeconomic adjustment ahead of EMU. As explained above, countries have to comply with the convergence criteria laid down in the Maastricht treaty in order to participate in EMU. The inflation and long-term interest rate criteria are likely to be met by a number of countries. But the fiscal criteria, limiting budget deficits and government debt levels, require budgetary adjustments such as raising taxes and cutting government spending, if key countries, including France and Germany, are to meet the criteria even on a liberal interpretation.

There are two big problems with general fiscal retrenchment of this kind. The first is that fiscal tightening has a long way to go before it delivers significantly lower budget deficits. This is because of the short-run multiplier process, both at home and internationally. Budget cuts, whether in the form of tax increases or cuts in public spending, tend to lower demand and therefore economic activity and income in the economy as a whole. Tax revenues tend therefore to fall, and transfer payments such as unemployment benefits and other income-related benefits tend to rise. The result is only a modest improvement in the budget deficit.

The recession of 1997-98?

When groups of countries engage in fiscal contraction together, as the European countries are now doing, the induced recession is all the deeper and the resulting improvement in deficits all the smaller. This is because contraction in one country reduces import demand, lowering exports of its trading partners, and thereby lowering activity and income in those export markets. In effect, the international multiplier exports recession. Since all countries are doing this together, the recession is deeper and budget deficits improve rather little. The implication is that the process of budget adjustment will have to be far-reaching if the Maastricht fiscal criteria are to be met, and the associated recession may be quite severe.

This leads to the second problem. A major recession would be an inauspicious start to monetary union. More significantly, it could derail the project; if recession leads electorates and governments to question the wisdom of EMU, then foreign exchange markets could see the weakening of political commitment to EMU as the basis for speculating against the project.

These doubts about the transition are significant, but they should not be seen as insoluble. The fiscal contraction could be offset by an appropriate relaxation of monetary policy, with the Bundesbank and EMI bringing interest rates down. (Note that German interest rates have indeed been coming down.) Such a relaxation need not threaten inflation, since overall demand growth would remain moderate: the expansion of demand due to the monetary relaxation would merely offset the contraction of demand due to fiscal retrenchment, and would not add to demand overall. Fiscal retrenchment therefore need not lead to recession, but merely to a rebalancing of monetary and fiscal policy.

The marginal "ins", such as Italy, Portugal and Spain, have already enjoyed an effective relaxation of monetary policy since their long-term and short-term interest rates have come down sharply as the markets have boosted their probability of participation. For these countries, fiscal retrenchment has been balanced in large part by monetary ease. The fall in rates has also greatly improved their fiscal position, by reducing interest payments on government debt. (Thus, for Italy, an interest-rate decline of one percentage point lowers government interest payments by approximately 1% of GDP within two years.) These countries are now in a virtuous circle of convergence. Indeed, if their interest rates slip to German levels, they will gain the double bonus of fiscal convergence and monetary stimulus. For them, the disaster will be failure to participate in EMU, which could see interest rates snap back, bringing recession and a widening fiscal deficit.

All eyes on the Bundesbank

As with the travails in 1992-93 of the EMS, what is required is that the Bundesbank look beyond its national brief and take a view of the fiscal-monetary mix across all the probable EMU "ins", providing lower interest rates if appropriate. It is uncertain whether the Bundesbank will feel moved to make this gesture. This leaves open the possibility that a Maastricht-engineered recession will upset the transition to EMU.

Figure 3.11
Long-term government bond yields

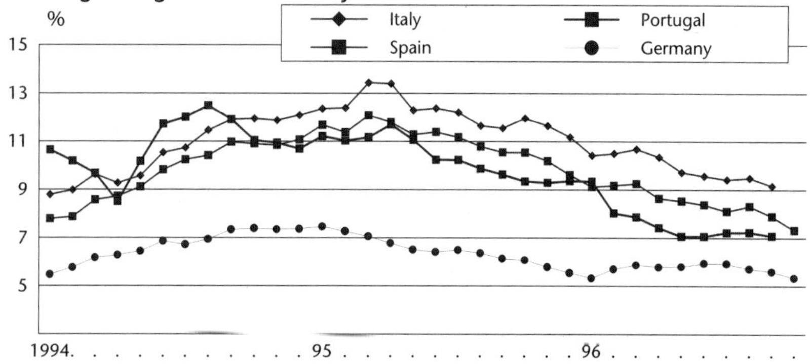

Chapter 4 The macroeconomic consequences of EMU

In this chapter, we examine the economic consequences of EMU in greater detail, looking at the pros and cons for macroeconomic performance in the EU.

Modestly lower transaction costs

Savings of money and time

One of the most obvious benefits from the introduction of the euro is the resulting ease of transactions across the EU. This will save both money and time. Estimates of the possible savings vary, but the usual range is around 0.2-0.5% of GDP. (In part, the range reflects uncertainty about the number of countries participating in EMU. Clearly the savings are greater, the bigger the number of participants, since the usefulness of the euro depends on how many people are using it.) This is not a negligible amount, but nor is it large, amounting to only one or two months' growth in GDP. Indeed, the costs of converting to the euro are likely to be appreciably higher than these savings. Although the conversion costs are one-off while the benefits are ongoing and permanent, the net transactions savings do not provide a strong reason for moving to the euro.

Eliminating exchange-rate volatility

EMU eliminates the possibility of exchange-rate variation within the EMU zone. If it is true that exchange rates move to help macroeconomic adjustment, this may well represent a cost of EMU. But if exchange rates more often move erratically and unsystematically in response to arbitrary speculation, exchange-rate volatility imposes a macroeconomic cost, and its elimination represents an advantage. Both views capture an aspect of the truth: exchange rates do tend to play a useful adjustment role, but also incorporate a large arbitrary and disruptive element. The more the latter predominates over the former, the greater the benefits of eliminating exchange-rate fluctuations through EMU.

Controlling inflation

For many proponents of EMU, an important advantage is the promised independence of the ECB in the conduct of European monetary policy, and the prospect that this independence will assure durably low inflation for the EMU area as a whole. For Germany, which has enjoyed low inflation for decades, the ECB can scarcely offer more on this front than the status quo. Indeed, the ECB's performance may not be as good as the Bundesbank's, for reasons that we will consider in a moment. These reservations probably apply also to those countries, such as Austria, France and the Netherlands, that have attached their currency to the D-mark and hence adopted the Bundesbank as their *de facto* central bank. For them, however, the creation of the ECB offers a voice in the conduct of monetary policy which they currently lack.

If the ECB has the will

The disinflation benefits will plainly be greatest for EMU countries that have not enjoyed stable low inflation hitherto. These include Ireland and the UK (were it to join) together with Italy, Portugal and Spain (were they to be allowed to participate). Low inflation implies low interest rates, both short-term and long-term, as the premiums for inflation and exchange-rate risk would be eliminated from interest rates. Three factors could, however, make the ECB's performance somewhat more erratic than the Bundesbank's.

- Day-to-day decisions on monetary policy will be made by the ECB's executive board, comprising six independent appointed experts, including the president and vice-president. It will be accountable to a governing council, which will have the governors of the central banks of the participating countries represented on it. There is a concern that, if and when the membership widens, the governors of central banks from more inflation-prone countries could take a less robust line on limiting inflation—even though those central banks will be independent. If this is so, a more inflationary bias could enter the conduct of monetary policy. In particular, this could happen if the political authority of the ECB were tested and led to compromises in the conduct of monetary policy—on inflation, for example—or equally importantly, on a high and rising level of unemployment. It is legitimate to ask at what level of pressure the ECB's political resolve might buckle, as even the resolve of the Bundesbank buckled at the time of German reunification. However, the Maastricht treaty requirement that central banks must be independent to participate in EMU acts as a safeguard against this inflationary risk.

- Unlike the Bundesbank, the ECB has a reputation to establish, and its actions may be scrutinised by the markets for some time before they are convinced about the ECB's anti-inflation credentials. A period of somewhat higher interest rates may be needed to demonstrate anti-inflation resolve. This in turn could reinforce internal dissent on the executive council.

- The ECB will set to work at the start of a wholly new monetary regime, namely EMU, which may well alter the workings of the joint monetary economy in significant and unpredictable ways. All central banks have to cope with such changes from time to time: examples include the shift in UK demand for money after financial markets were liberalised in the 1980s, and the change in the circulation and use of D-marks after German unification. At such times, policymakers can lose their bearings, and the conduct of monetary policy can become volatile. The shift associated with EMU could be quite profound, and monetary relationships that held in the past may have quite limited relevance to the future conduct of policy. In having to cope with such a shift at its launch, the ECB will enjoy the monetary equivalent of a baptism of fire.

On balance, it seems likely that the ECB will be able to establish a record and reputation for conducting monetary policy in a sound manner. But this may take time, and in the meantime euro monetary policy, and the capital and currency markets' judgement of it, may prove erratic.

Government borrowing

A big concern of rigorous-minded EMU doubters is that EMU will ease the market constraints on excess borrowing by profligate governments, leading to excessive borrowing and an EMU "debt trap". Germans, in particular, worry that they will be called upon in EMU to bail out high-borrowing governments. This concern motivated the formulation of the Maastricht fiscal convergence criteria and the later stability and growth pact, which reflects Germany's determination that the convergence criteria should be interpreted strictly. It also motivated the drafters of the Maastricht treaty to incorporate the no bail-out clause, which precludes the ECB from bailing out debt-ridden bankrupt governments by buying their debt.

Two kinds of excess

This argument needs some unpicking to make sense of it. Two distinct types of government debt problems may arise.

- **Unsustainable debt.** This happens when governments borrow in a way that cannot continue indefinitely, since it leads to ever-larger accumulations of debt and eventual insolvency. An example is Greece, where debt levels have been rising steadily over the past 15 years, in a way that will eventually have to come to a radical end.

- **High but sustainable debt.** This is where governments are able to service their debt indefinitely (ie, the debts are sustainable) but the levels are unduly high. An example is Belgium, which has sustained a debt level of 130-140% of GDP since the early 1980s.

The two problems give rise to different concerns. If a government participating in EMU gets into a debt trap, there could be pressure on other member governments to bail it out, providing subsidies to help service the debt, or taking over responsibility for the debt itself. For example, say the worriers, Germany and France will surely be unwilling or unable to stand aside and see the Italian government collapse in the chaos of financial insolvency, with all the implied disruption to economic, social and civil society.

If the debt is merely high, rather than unsustainable, there should be no need to bail out other governments. Instead, the concern is that if some governments are able to borrow heavily, this will push up the general cost of borrowing: high government debt across the EMU zone will push up real interest rates on euro borrowing to the detriment of all, and to the particular chagrin of thrifty governments.

The role of market discipline

Although these concerns are real, their underlying logic is not watertight. A single currency does not automatically lead to a greater capacity for profligate governments to borrow, any more than a single currency in, say, the UK makes it easier for profligate individuals or organisations to borrow pounds. Financial markets judge credit risk, and penalise borrowers who represent a poor risk. They can do this by reducing the value of a currency in which a debt is denominated, or by marking down the value of the debt itself.

In EMU, different governments will be required to pay different rates of interest on their euro debt, depending on their credit rating. High-debt governments are likely to face a risk premium (on top of the risk-free real interest rate) that reflects the greater risk of holding their debt. If they appear to be running a fiscal policy that lets debt spiral upwards, they will again be penalised with higher risk premiums.

This process can be observed in the USA. Different state governments have to pay different interest rates on their debt, according to their creditworthiness. Note also that high default-risk premiums on government debt need not imply similar risk premiums on private debt. An Italian company, say, could be considered an entirely safe risk in the euro-denominated debt market even if its government were not. Indeed the common currency makes it easier for sound private borrowers to be distinguished from their profligate governments: they are no longer tarred with the national currency. Thus one of the leading credit agencies has announced that within EMU an individual European company could be given a higher credit rating than its government, which is currently not possible.

Of course, this market discipline may sometimes fail. Some argue that markets may ignore accumulating debt problems for some time, and then suddenly turn against risky debt, moving abruptly from calm to crisis. Or suppose the markets expect other governments to bail out any member of EMU that gets into difficulties. In that case, there would be no risk premium on the debt of profligate governments. Overborrowing, and a subsequent debt crisis, would then be all the more likely. Hence the German concern that their government will end up paying for the profligacy of others.

Would it be possible to resist the pressure for a bail-out? When New York City ran into debt problems in the early 1980s, neither federal nor state government came to its aid. And if a bail-out were motivated by concern over the social and political consequences of a debt crisis, then this could apply as much within today's EU, particularly now that its citizens are no longer "captive lenders" obliged to hold their wealth in their respective national currencies. In practice, when governments face debt problems they do not go bankrupt—they adopt tough fiscal measures to resolve the crisis. In the grip of a single ECB which will no longer tide over an indebted government with bank credit (printed money), the pressure on the profligate to do what is necessary will be all the greater.

How to strengthen the constraints

In fact, the ECB will be expressly forbidden to finance government budget deficits. True, it has to engage in open-market operations in euros, buying and selling euro debt in order to control the euro money supply. In the absence of any European federal debt, such operations will take place in the euro debt of the national governments. But in so doing, the ECB faces a choice as to which national debt it should buy or sell. The ECB could adopt a mechanical rule, buying and selling the debt of the national governments in fixed proportions, perhaps reflecting their economies' weight in the EU's GDP. Or it could adopt a more prudent strategy of holding only the debt of countries with "conservative" fiscal policies. By declining to buy the debt of profligate countries, and/or by selling the debt of countries whose policies become imprudent, the ECB could provide a useful signal to the market, thereby reinforcing its discipline. Whether the ECB will adopt such a strategy, even supposing it would be allowed to, remains to be seen.

But this may not be enough

So much for unsustainable debts. Paradoxically, the problem of high but sustainable debts is potentially more difficult. True, if all governments increased their debt (as a proportion of GDP) to Belgium's level, then the general level of interest rates would rise. This is because investors wish to keep a balanced portfolio of money, fixed-interest debt, equities and other assets. To persuade them to increase their holdings of debt substantially, the return on debt must improve. It may not matter much elsewhere if a small country such as Belgium is deeply in debt, but if all countries, including the large ones, were in that position, European real interest rates could rise sharply. This would make it harder to finance investment and would worsen the prospects for long-term growth.

The argument has some force. But note that the level of debt in the EU is already high. In principle as well as in practice, it is unclear whether floating exchange rates or monetary union do more to encourage prudent public finance. With a single currency, it is argued, governments can borrow partly at other governments' expense, because their extra demands on the capital market force up the interest rate across Europe, rather than forcing up merely their own interest rate. This financial "externality", as it has been called, will encourage more borrowing. But the effect is unlikely to be large, because the borrowing of no one country is very great in relation to Europe's public borrowing in the aggregate. And another factor acts to offset this incentive, such as it is. With a single currency, governments know that they will be unable to reduce the burden of their debts by letting inflation rise (an option that many of Europe's national governments have used in the past). In the end, they will have to finance their borrowing through explicit taxes, not through the hidden tax of inflation. This should help to encourage sound public finance.

This is not to argue against restraints on borrowing, for current levels of borrowing are too high. But it suggests that EMU, in itself, is unlikely to worsen the problem, and may well ameliorate it.

The spectre of unfunded pension liabilities

An additional concern is that government deficits and debts offer a less than complete picture of public finances. Governments may have hidden assets, such as publicly owned land or other natural resources, which may well appreciate in real terms. Equally, governments may have hidden liabilities. These may include potential additional demands on public services by an ageing population, as well as unfunded public pension liabilities. A true picture of the government's fiscal position can only be obtained by taking all these factors into account, not just by concentrating on the budget deficit and debt ratios of the Maastricht convergence criteria.

The spotlight has recently focused on the high level of public pension liabilities in many continental European countries. Current pension arrangements in several of these countries imply a level of transfer from the working to the retired population in the first half of the next century that is likely to be unsustainable, unless European economic growth takes off dramatically. Thus the OECD has estimated the capitalised (or net present value) cost of current pension arrangements to be 98% of GDP in France, 113% of GDP in Italy and 139% of GDP in Germany, compared with a mere 19% in the UK.

These calculations are fraught with difficulty, and subject to a wide margin of error. Comparatively small changes in trend growth rates and in the assumed discount rate, derived from assumed real interest rates into the future, can change the estimates appreciably. What cannot be denied, however, is that the numbers point to a real public policy dilemma. Those who argue that these prospective liabilities (and assets) should figure in the convergence criteria for EMU have a point. However, the prospective liability numbers are probably too uncertain to figure in any treaty provision. Furthermore, the convergence criteria would have to be framed very differently, were these liabilities to be included.

Difficult choices

Critics of EMU in the UK have raised the possibility that UK membership of EMU might result in UK taxpayers having to share the cost of funding French, Italian and German pensions. Does this fear have any basis in fact? What is clear is that, if current projections are borne out (and, notwithstanding their sensitivity, they are as good as any), European governments will face difficult choices from the following options.

- to raise taxes to finance future pensions, which would be met with political resistance from wage-earners;
- to slash pension rights, which would cause a backlash from pensioners;
- to borrow heavily, in breach of the Maastricht guidelines, which would thrust the governments into an ever-tightening debt trap;
- to look to other governments to bail them out so that they can meet their pension liabilities.

The fourth possibility is the scenario that EMU sceptics fear. Yet it seems unlikely to materialise. The Maastricht treaty and stability pact are designed to preclude the bailing out of profligate governments. There is no reason to suppose that this principle will be overthrown in respect of pensions. Indeed, it is not unreasonable to assume that individual governments will eventually sort out their pension problems for themselves, scaling down pension commitments to a level that can realistically be funded from taxes. That is what the UK did in the 1980s when faced with the same problem. It is not evident why EMU, with its additional constraints on borrowing in the form of the stability pact, should make this less likely.

However, EMU optimists must recognise the real risk that the stability pact will not stem the tide; that governments will respond too little and too late to these pressures, and in the end will resort to borrowing to fund a large part of their pension liabilities. If that happens, it will be bad news for the euro zone, which will became a high-debt, high-interest rate region, to the detriment of investment, growth and prosperity.

The growing mood of fiscal realism in European countries suggests that this threat may be averted. Certainly, Maastricht, with its emphasis on fiscal convergence criteria and the stability pact, has helped in this respect. But the crucial point is that the threat of excessive government borrowing to fund state pensions is present, with or without EMU. And excessive borrowing will raise the real cost of borrowing, both in the borrowing country and more generally, because of the integration of international capital markets. Thus the countries of Europe, Asia and other parts of the world were obliged to share the cost of financing excessive US borrowing in the 1980s, despite having separate currencies. If early in the next century EMU countries plunge into debt, other European countries will pay a price, whether or not they participate in EMU.

In the end, therefore, the pensions issue can be reduced to the same single question we have addressed before: will EMU encourage or discourage participating countries from excessive borrowing? The institutional design is clearly aimed at discouragement. But as we have said, in practice much will depend on the actual operations of the ECB and the perceptions of the market. EMU may well prove to be harsh on the profligate, but the pensions spectre that haunts EMU sceptics has yet to be laid to rest.

Managing the economic cycle

Proponents of EMU argue that giving up the exchange rate as an instrument of economic policy prevents governments from resorting to the soft option of devaluation. The much vaunted independence of monetary policy has meant, in the experience of the UK and other countries, the freedom to inflate faster and to engage in a progressive devaluation of the currency.

Against this, critics rightly say that EMU means giving up an important economic policy instrument. Outside EMU, the UK has the freedom to set interest rates appropriate to its domestic economic circumstances, and in particular to the ups and downs of its own economic cycle, independently of policy in other European countries. This independent monetary policy will be reflected in movements of the exchange rate, but such movements can support, not undermine, domestic policy. Proponents of this view note that the 1992 sterling devaluation helped to lay the basis for subsequent growth with continued low inflation; critics note that the 1976 fall of sterling was much less supportive, and that exchange-rate volatility can be excessive. Inside EMU, monetary policy cannot respond to the particular and distinct circumstances of a particular national economy; instead euro monetary policy will be set to reflect average circumstances across the countries participating in EMU.

Is the UK out of synch?

The loss of monetary policy as an independent tool for dealing with economic cycles would not matter if two conditions were satisfied.

- If economic cycles in the different EMU countries coincided.
- If the effects of a given monetary policy were the same in each of the EMU countries.

OCA ⊃ Shocks

In fact neither condition applies. Evidence on the cycle across the European economies shows both a common element, due to aggregate shocks affecting all economies together, and a national element due to so-called asymmetric shocks. An example of an aggregate shock would be a fall in global (ie, non-European) demand; this would affect every European exporter in broadly the same way, even though the severity would vary from case to case. A good example of an asymmetric shock is an increase in the price of oil: the UK, as an oil exporter, gains; other European countries, net oil importers, lose. The economies at the heart of the EU (Germany, France, and the Benelux countries) seem more closely integrated and somewhat less susceptible to asymmetric shocks. Nonetheless, giving up an independent monetary policy does carry a cost on this account.

The evidence on monetary policy in the EU also shows a differential effect. This is not surprising, given the different structures of European financial systems. In particular, UK households are much more sensitive to interest rates than their German equivalents. They tend to borrow heavily (mainly in the form of mortgage finance) and at a variable rate of interest. German households generally owe less in relation to their income, and more of the debt is at a fixed interest rate.

The consequence is that, if the UK and Germany both participated in EMU, and the ECB raised interest rates to curb demand or inflation in the EMU zone, the impact would fall disproportionately on the UK economy. Conversely, UK demand would benefit disproportionately from the expansionary effect of the ECB cutting euro interest rates. A common euro monetary policy would result in a stronger cycle in the UK relative to Germany, because of the differential impact of monetary policy.

Integration may bring convergence

Yet these arguments should not be overstated. With growing integration among Europe's economies, the significance of differential shocks may well diminish. Moreover, differences in the structure and level of debt across countries are largely a product of different economic circumstances and history, and with time these will dwindle. Thus, for instance, the high level of personal sector debt in the UK reflects the benefits of investing in housing in a chronically inflation-prone economy, where the government gave generous tax incentives to invest in bricks and mortar. Such incentives have now been largely withdrawn and low inflation prevails.

The UK economy's response to monetary policy may therefore become more like that of Germany over time. Reductions in debt are already apparent, and fixed-interest debt is gaining in popularity relative to variable-rate debt and could be encouraged further. But the adjustment will be slow: it will take many years for household debt in the UK to fall to German levels, in relation to income. In the meantime, the UK personal sector will respond much more sensitively to changes in monetary policy. This is a good argument for the UK remaining outside EMU so that it can apply an independent monetary policy appropriate to its particular economic circumstances.

If countries experience differential shocks that reduce income, output and employment in their economy relative to that of other participants in EMU, their economies will be forced to adjust in one way or another. Within EMU, the exchange-rate weapon will be ruled out, so adjustment will be forced through other channels. There are two primary ones:

- wages can fall;
- workers can move.

Adjustment through wages

If an economy falls behind in productivity, an adjustment mechanism is needed to ensure that it remains competitive. One such mechanism is an adjustment of relative wages and/or living standards. In the long run, this is the same real adjustment as is implied by devaluation: instead of the exchange rate falling, raising prices for a given level of wages, wages fall for a given exchange rate and price level. But the short-term consequences of the process of adjustment will be different in the two cases.

If nominal wages adjust downwards only sluggishly, then reducing living standards through lower nominal wages will be much more costly in terms of unemployment than the alternative of devaluing the exchange rate. In this case, monetary independence outside EMU retains considerable benefit. However, the empirical evidence on wage determination, uncertain though it is, seems to suggest that Europe exhibits sluggish real wages, not sluggish nominal wages: nominal wages tend to keep in line with prices, so that real wages show little tendency to fall even in periods of high unemployment. (In this respect Europe is very different from America.) If this is true of both upward and downward adjustments (the evidence on this point is not firm), then adjustment within EMU may be no more costly than adjustment outside.

Labour mobility

The other main adjustment mechanism is labour mobility. If one country in EMU suffers a sustained recession, then the resulting unemployment may well induce an outflow of labour. Simple market economics would suggest that the movement of labour from a country with a relatively low demand for labour to one with a higher demand would bring the demand for labour within EMU into better overall balance.

This hope is for many people one of the weakest points in the pro-EMU argument. Language and loyalty to nation and the national way of life prevent many people from moving around Europe in search of a job in the way that they move within the USA. And the labour that does tend to move is often the more flexible and capable part of the workforce, adding to rather than solving the problem for the depressed country that is losing workers. This may change, if perhaps only gradually, but the highly mobile international workers of Italy, Spain and Portugal may well provide a pointer to the European future. Until then, the main burden of adjustment in any country with above-average unemployment will be downward pressure on wages.

However, there are reasons for taking a more optimistic view on the issue of EMU and country-specific shocks. The states of the USA tend to be much more specialised in production than do the states of the EU. This makes them more susceptible to serious asymmetric or state-specific shocks. The need for adjustment, whether through labour mobility or fiscal transfers, is therefore much greater. With less specialisation, European countries need to rely less on such adjustments. This may, of course, change over time, particularly with the further development of the single market. But such development may well go in parallel with higher labour mobility and increased fiscal transfers. In the meantime, the proposed EMU may be less susceptible to asymmetric shocks than its critics often suppose.

The future of the single market

Some argue that the single market is the crucial achievement of the EU, and that EMU is irrelevant to its completion. This position, often taken by British commentators, considers the single currency as a distraction from the more important task of deeper economic integration in the EU.

The coming rift between the "ins" and "outs"

Reinforcing this assertion is a growing worry in EU countries that are unlikely to join EMU that non-participation may lead to discrimination by the "ins" against the "outs", using a variety of devices to impede the access of firms to the European market. Although the principles of the single market are enshrined in treaty, there is some talk of loopholes that will allow covert discrimination to take place, with the authorities in Brussels and Luxembourg turning a blind eye. Critics of the European Court argue that its judgments are often political, not to be defended on strictly legal grounds. (The same point can, of course, be made about aspects of, say, the UK judiciary or the US Supreme Court.) If protectionist measures are part of a broader political current to "build Europe", then it is perhaps more likely that the Court's judgment will flow with the stream.

Economic theory suggests that the damage done by any such protectionism would fall as much upon the excluders within the circle of EMU as upon the excluded in, say, Italy and the UK. Unfortunately the political process is usually a poor student of economics—otherwise the history of global trade would have been very different—and theory will do little to avert such retaliation. A better hope lies in recent EU experience. Despite some big devaluations within the single market during the 1990s, most notably by Italy and the UK, complaints about competitive devaluation have not so far been transformed into protectionist deeds, although they did sour French attitudes to the completion of the Uruguay round of trade negotiations.

Strong-currency governments may take a rather different view under EMU. Where once they freely decided to preserve their parities with the D-mark, they will now have thrown away the key and may be more resentful of governments that have kept their options open. It seems possible that EMU in a partial form will lead to some discrimination between the "ins" and the "outs" (or perhaps just the voluntary "outs"). This prospect is an important argument against EMU as a whole. But, to make the choice more complicated, it is also an argument for participation by countries that might otherwise stand aside, if the partial EMU project goes ahead regardless.

The possibility of discrimination arises from the operation of the political process. All governments are subject to lobbying by industrial pressure groups seeking to obtain measures that exclude overseas competitors. Such lobbying is more likely to be effective when it can combine with a wider political current, as with the recent alliance between protectionist sentiment and the environmental lobby. In this case the alliance will not be with the force of greener sentiment, but against the forces of euro-doubt.

There are four main ways in which the "ins" could discriminate against the "outs":

- by exploiting loopholes in existing single market directives applying to trade in goods and services;
- by devising forms of market opening in new, currently closed areas (for example, European gas and electricity markets) that work to the disadvantage of the "outs";
- by failing to represent the interests of the "outs" as strongly (recognising that negotiations often arrive at a balancing of national interests);
- in the financial area, by exploiting a clause in the investment services directive which permits national discrimination in the provision of financial services as a counter-party to the state, the central bank or other national bodies fulfilling similar roles.

Two sets of rules?

This last is a provision with quite a wide potential reach. For example, it might apply to government-bond dealing insofar as it is part of the conduct of monetary policy by the central bank. It could provide the legal basis for devising one set of rules for the "ins" and another, more restrictive set of rules for the "outs". There is also a more generally drafted provision in article 19 of the Maastricht treaty that gives member states the right to act "in the general good", which is left undefined and therefore subject to legal interpretation. This phrase appears in quite a lot of European legislation and has been interpreted by the European Court so far generally in a way that has been supportive of the evolution of the single market. If the Court chose to interpret EMU as being "in the general good", then this interpretation could be used to support measures that, for example, ran counter to the single market but were considered to be in the interests of EMU.

Ultimately these issues will be determined by the institutions of the European Union, and the views of the Commission and the Council of Ministers will be a very important influence. This accounts for unease over the UK's position as a likely "voluntary out". If seen by the other member states as an opting-out from the mainstream of the EU, this might well diminish the UK's influence over key issues, both now and in the future, and could mean that the UK's national interests will weigh less in the balance. Appeal to European law provides some defence against this, but the defence is insecure. The UK's à la carte approach to Europe has some undoubted advantages, but it also has its costs.

Fiscal federalism

In Chapter 2, we discussed whether the move to EMU requires a move to a much more centralised form of federation. Our provisional answer, based on the historical evidence, was that it does not. (Although we noted that the monetary unions that emerged in the last century did evolve politically towards federation, we also noted that the intensity of federation is a matter on which the EU as a whole can make a choice.) This is not to suggest that the EU will not evolve in a more centralised direction, but simply to say that it can choose otherwise.

Here we consider a much more specific question: does EMU require for its survival a system of interstate transfers, otherwise known as "fiscal federalism"? This has been argued by many, including the influential McDougall report, which suggested that monetary union in Europe was not viable unless at least 20% of government taxes in the EU were available for redistribution through the budget of the EU as a whole.

In support of this position, one can observe that all existing monetary unions involve fiscal transfers of at least this sort of magnitude. These run the gamut from centralised European states such as Germany or France, where the degree of redistribution is very high, through less centralised states such as the USA, to the loosest example, namely Switzerland, where approximately 20% of income is redistributed at the margin through the central budget.

This redistribution happens automatically through the federal element of the tax systems: although a number of taxes and transfers operate only at the state level, the existence of a federal tax/transfer system in addition means that transfers take place automatically from jurisdictions in boom to those in recession. Thus if one part of the monetary union moves into recession, its tax payments (linked to income and sales) to the centre will fall and federal benefit payments will rise; while the opposite will happen for those regions in boom. All that is required for this to happen is that some tax or transfer mechanisms work at the level of the monetary union as a whole.

It is important to remember that these are all examples of mature monetary unions. In the era of small government up to the second world war, however, they existed for many decades without major fiscal transfers of this kind. This could be taken as evidence that while monetary unions tend over time to foster the political and social conditions for fiscal transfers, such transfers are not necessary for the operation of a monetary union.

Why fiscal transfers matter

For a monetary union, or any other international arrangement of this kind, to endure, it must be in the interests of all countries to maintain their membership. For some countries, it may make sense at a certain point (for example, in the late 1990s) to join such a union. There will be costs and benefits, but for such countries, let us suppose, the expected benefits outweigh the expected costs: the benefits of lower inflation, greater economic integration and reduced exchange-rate volatility outweigh the loss of monetary sovereignty and the associated reduced capacity to respond to asymmetric shocks.

The trouble is, this calculation may be upset by changed circumstances. Any decision of this kind, which averages over many possible states of the world, runs the risk of turning out to be wrong if some particular state of the world (however improbable it may seem) comes about. Suppose an adverse shock such as a major recession hits one country in EMU but not the others. It may lead that country to reconsider whether its membership of EMU is wise, even if the basis of the original calculation was right; that is, the original decision was sensible, but the country was just unlucky. If the adverse shock is not great, then the country may simply accept its bad luck (though there may be a fall in the stock of those responsible for taking the country into EMU). But if the shock is large enough, then it may pay the country to consider withdrawal from EMU, even if the costs of doing that are large.

What has all this to do with fiscal federalism? If fiscal transfers are in place, then the effect of the adverse shock pushing the country into recession will be offset in part by transfers from the rest of the union. (By the same token, transfers in the other direction would moderate a boom.) With transfers of this kind, countries would be much less likely to regard EMU as a constraint when faced by serious adverse shocks. This leads to two conclusions.

- A monetary union can persist without fiscal transfers. If the expected net benefits from EMU are sufficiently large, and the costs of withdrawal are high, then only in the face of very severe adverse shocks will countries be tempted even to consider withdrawal. EMU might exist for a considerable time before such a shock occurs, indeed for long enough to seem a fixture in the changing world of economic, social and political arrangements.

- Within EMU there may be pressures, nonetheless, for the evolution of a system of fiscal transfers. When adverse shocks arise, there will be a tendency for the system to be adjusted so as to respond to emerging political concerns and to ensure that all members remain content with EMU participation. A system of fiscal transfers would help in this while appearing fair to all members of the monetary union. The gradual introduction of such a system would be a natural outcome of the workings of the political marketplace through a process of sequential bargaining.

In this discussion, it is important to appreciate that the transfers in question relate to the cyclical component of national performance, rather than to sustained differences in performance. There is no reason why the rich countries in EMU, such as Germany, should compensate the poorer ones. Since the poorer countries are likely to remain poorer, whether inside or outside EMU, this is not a factor that need influence the cohesion or otherwise of EMU. The cyclical differences are what matter. These can be accommodated without any net transfers over time from rich countries to poor ones. Countries would gain in recessions and pay in booms, with the flows balancing over the cycle.

The scale of the problem

What would this mean in practice? The EU currently takes an average of around 1.4% of EU tax revenues, resulting in a total annual budget of Ecu82bn. This seems low, relative to the 20% quoted as the minimum by the McDougall report. But there is an important distinction between the marginal and average redistribution. An overall budget of 2% of the EU's GDP could, on reasonable assumptions, be used to effect redistributions of 20% at the margin between EMU members. But this would require the budget to be targeted specifically for this purpose, and not be used, as at present, for sustaining inefficient European agriculture and heavy industry.

An important point about EMU in its partial form is that the fiscal transfers that are relevant are between the participants in EMU, not all the members of the EU. Unless all members of the EU eventually join EMU, our analysis suggests that the pressure will be for the emergence of a system of fiscal transfers within the EMU bloc, rather than across the EU as a whole. This reinforces the prospect (suggested already by the need for an "ins" subset of Ecofin) that, unless all EU members eventually join, EMU will divide the Union into two increasingly different parts.

The danger of excessive rigidity

It will be a considerable time before fiscal federalism follows in the wake of EMU, if ever. There are no plans for such fiscal transfers, and the political consensus required for their introduction is absent. Thus EMU will have to operate without fiscal transfers. As we have seen, the historical examples suggest that it can do so. But there are risks, particularly if the operation of fiscal policy by national governments is unduly constrained.

EMU will remove the independent use of monetary policy and associated exchange-rate flexibility from the arsenal of weapons available to national governments to tackle the ups and downs of their particular national economic cycle. This places greater weight on remaining instruments, notably fiscal policy. But the stability pact, motivated by the admirable objective of discouraging excessive borrowing by national governments, has the side consequence of reducing the flexibility of national fiscal policy over the cycle.

Thus, as explained in Chapter 3, the stability pact sets out fines for deficits in excess of 3% of GDP, unless corrective action is put in place to bring the deficit back down below 3%. Yet in recession, a larger deficit helps to mitigate recessionary tendencies. Allowing automatic fiscal stabilisers (ie the natural tendency for the deficit to rise and fall with the cycle, thereby mitigating it) requires movements of the deficit up (and down) of some 3-4% of GDP. So unless national governments aim at a balanced budget or surplus, the deficit limit of 3% could well prevent the proper working of fiscal stabilisers. This means that governments would be required to raise taxes, or cut government spending, as the economy moves into recession, thereby exacerbating the downturn. That could well weaken overall support for the single currency, once the contractionary consequences of the stability pact are appreciated.

To be sure, the stability pact, as agreed, incorporates a let-out for severe downturns of more than 2%, with ministerial discretion on fines for downturns of more than 0.75%. But even a smaller fall in output, if sustained, can be very painful in terms of unemployment, as France has experienced over the past few years. The stability pact therefore poses a dilemma: in aiming to prevent high and rising debt levels, it constrains responsible flexibility of fiscal policy over the cycle. The consequence could be a bumpier ride for the European economy, as all the national levers of policy are disabled. This points to a need for the stability pact to be interpreted as flexibly as possible, especially for those governments whose trend debt ratio is low and stable. It also suggests that a better stability pact would emphasise the trend and overall level of national debt ratios, rather than the particular level of the fiscal deficit, which is so subject to cyclical influences.

Interest rates

Where inflation has become a habit, if not a way of life, one immediate effect of EMU will be lower nominal interest rates. In high-inflation economies, interest rates incorporate an element to reflect the erosion of the real value of money. If the ECB delivers low inflation and the markets expect it to keep on doing so, nominal interest rates will drop. This is to the immediate advantage of companies and individuals that are debtors, lowering the front-end loading that goes with high nominal interest rates, lowering interest payments and improving cash flow. But in net present value terms, a reduction in nominal interest rates that merely reflects lower inflation will not alter the overall burden of debt. It will simply redistribute the burden from the near term to the longer term. (When inflation was rapid in the UK, high interest rates placed an initially heavy burden on mortgage borrowers, but this diminished quickly. Now, with a lower inflation rate, the initial burden is lighter, but it remains significant for longer because the real value of debt is eroded more slowly.)

Eliminating a risk premium

However, it is possible that interest rates will be lower in real terms as well—lower, that is, after adjusting for inflation. Interest rates in high-inflation countries often incorporate a currency- or inflation-risk element. In 1994-95 markets seemed to be expecting UK inflation of around 3.5%; in fact, inflation averaged 2.5%. Thus UK borrowers were paying a 1% risk premium on short-term interest rates. Longer-term inflation expectations over the next decade signalled an expected inflation rate in the 4-4.5% range. With a single currency, this risk premium is likely to be eliminated, reducing the burden of servicing debt. This will be good not only for companies and individuals with heavy debts; but also for longer-term investment.

Note one possible effect on the other side. If countries in EMU pile up heavy debts, as some fear, this could push up euro real interest rates, offsetting the gain on currency risk. We considered this earlier, concluding that such an outcome is unlikely to result directly from EMU.

A new kind of exchange-rate uncertainty

EMU is intended to eliminate exchange-rate uncertainty. It will clearly achieve that objective within the euro zone. But there are serious concerns that, at least for an extended transitional period, it will generate more, not less, instability between the euro and other currencies than we have seen between the D-mark and other currencies in the past. This matters for the countries within the euro zone, since they have significant trade with countries outside the zone, both within Europe and elsewhere. It would also matter for non-European countries, particularly since it may induce instability in non-European cross-rates.

How might EMU induce instability in exchange rates? There are two principal routes.

1. EMU may result in a "dollar overhang", partly because the pooling of reserves among the EMU participants leads overall to a reduced need for reserves—especially dollars—and partly because of the increased use of the euro in international trade. This would lead to a fall in the dollar against the euro, as international reserve portfolios were adjusted.

The Japanese concern is that an appreciation of the euro against the dollar will lead to a sharper rise in the yen against the dollar (and hence an appreciation of the yen against the euro, not just the dollar), since this has been the usual pattern in the past. That is certainly a possibility, though past patterns may not be a good guide to the effect of an unprecedented event such as the introduction of a new European currency. But if it occurs, Japanese industry may find itself once again having to adjust to a very high exchange rate, forcing further hollowing-out of Japanese industry and its transfer overseas. Because of so-called "J-curve" effects, an appreciating yen usually also leads to an increase in the bilateral trade surplus that Japan runs with the USA. If this happens, the result could easily be renewed and heightened tensions between America and Japan over trade.

2. Monetary policy may be badly conducted. The ECB will be untried in international financial markets, and it will have to establish its reputation. The learning process may involve errors and uncertainties, and this fact may be reflected in fluctuations of the euro. Even more seriously, critics of EMU can argue with force that there are weaknesses, potentially serious ones, in the institutional architecture of EMU. They point especially to two things.

- The unqualified political independence of the ECB. The conduct of monetary policy requires political legitimacy, but the Maastricht treaty provides no obvious means by which the ECB can gain it. Other central banks around the world, including the Bundesbank, are politically accountable.

- The role of Ecofin (notably in setting exchange-rate policy), and the resulting scope for conflict with the ECB. There is always the possibility of conflict between monetary and fiscal policy when these are set by different agencies, and this can become a testing political issue. Especially if it is unable to establish its legitimacy, the ECB may find itself on the losing side of any such arguments.

Imagine an ECB under pressure

To illustrate this possibility, consider the following. Five years after its creation, EMU has not resulted in the prosperity that its advocates envisaged. Unemployment remains high across the EMU zone, and continues to climb in some regions. Criticism of the project is rife, and opponents of EMU are winning electoral support. Opinion in Ecofin increasingly swings to the view that monetary policy needs to be laxer, despite possible inflationary consequences, in order to stimulate the economy of the euro zone and price euro-zone goods back into world markets through depreciation. Ecofin increasingly expresses this view publicly in opposition to the ECB's stern restatement of the need for continued tight monetary policy. Changes of national government bring to power politicians who had no role in choosing the members of the ECB's executive board. The bank's legitimacy is challenged not just by opposition parties but by national governments.

How does the ECB respond? Just as important, how do financial markets expect the ECB to respond? Their expectations will influence how the euro moves against other currencies, as well as movements in cross-rates between third currencies, such as the dollar:yen rate.

Perhaps EMU will work well, and such tensions will not emerge. If they do, they could plainly destabilise exchange rates. The markets may form the judgement that, faced with political opposition, the ECB will relax its monetary stance. This will lead to a fall in the euro. If the ECB then shows signs of confounding this expectation, the euro would rise again. Inherent in such conflicts is the possibility of a roller-coaster ride for the foreign exchanges. Far from creating exchange-rate stability, EMU could destabilise exchange rates beyond the EMU zone. It is even possible, on these assumptions, that members of EMU will experience greater overall exchange-rate instability than at present.

These transitional problems are not insuperable. A well-managed ECB could find solutions to the technical issues, and the political forces may develop in a benign way. Predictions that EMU will necessarily fail on these grounds are likely to be proved wrong. But the risk that technical problems and volatility will undermine EMU cannot be dismissed.

Chapter 5 EMU and business

A single European currency will have important consequences for European business. In Chapters 6 and 7 we look at the specific consequences for financial businesses. In this we examine the implications of EMU for businesses in general. Much of the analysis and the conclusions apply also to financial companies, such as insurance companies and mortgage and other lenders.

Advantages: lower costs, less risk and more competition

How businesses will gain

For business, a single European currency offers three main benefits.

- **Lower costs of managing cash.** For companies operating across national boundaries in Europe, it eliminates the costs of converting money from one national currency to another within the EMU zone. These costs are quite small for big companies, which enjoy benefits of scale, but may be more significant for small and medium-sized companies. These often lack the expertise for proper cash and foreign-exchange management: such expertise is expensive to contract out, and the scale of activity does not warrant appointing an in-house expert. A single currency eliminates conversion losses and simplifies cash management across the euro zone.

- **Less currency risk.** Within Europe, currency risk would be entirely eliminated. The need to hedge business transactions is likewise eliminated within the euro zone, and is therefore restricted to the dollar, yen and other non-euro currencies. Clearly the possible benefits of this are greater, the larger the number of countries participating in EMU. The benefits are also greater for companies whose trade is mainly in European markets. For companies whose trade is more internationally dispersed, the benefits of eliminating intra-European currency uncertainty may be small.

- **Bigger markets.** Companies will face a much larger, more integrated market across Europe. Customers will more readily purchase across national boundaries, unimpeded by the complexities of different currencies and the risk of exchange-rate variation. By eliminating the exchange-rate factor, companies will compete head-on without the currency barrier. Price lists will be increasingly pan-European as currency risk disappears. The only remaining barriers to crossborder trade of any significance will be non-monetary factors.

The more competitive market that this creates will pose both threats and opportunities. The efficient, customer-oriented company will have the opportunities of operating across a much larger customer base, whether as a large or niche player. But the inefficient or unresponsive company will find itself under pressure from the more intense competition. The resulting rationalisation of European industries will see winners and losers. But the customer will benefit through price reductions and improved service.

In addition there may be macroeconomic benefits, as discussed in Chapter 4. The possible gains in lower inflation and greater investment must be balanced against the possible costs of higher unemployment in weaker economies deprived of the exchange-rate instrument. We discuss these points no further here, except to note that if EMU yields significant macroeconomic costs then these could easily outweigh the potential benefits that we consider here; and by the same token if EMU yields important macroeconomic benefits, then these could easily swamp the possible costs that we discuss below.

A closer look at currency risk

The gain from lower currency risk is often questioned. It is argued that companies can hedge their exchange-rate exposure easily and cheaply through financial markets. Hedging through the forward and swap markets is straightforward, with margins for such transactions measured in decimal points of percentages. Since hedging against exchange risk is so simple, the benefits of eliminating such risk through a single currency cannot be significant.

This frequently advanced argument rests on a false assumption: that it makes sense for companies to hedge their currency exposure in full. This would be so only in the hypothetical case where currency uncertainty was the only risk facing the company. Full hedging would then make sense, provided that the cost of hedging was not too dear, a condition that is likely to be met in efficient financial markets. In practice, however, full hedging is unattractive for at least two reasons.

First, it is impractical. For a multidivision company, full hedging requires a netting across all the divisions of the company of the different exchange-rate exposures. This creates major problems if payment to those working in different divisions is based on recorded results in order to provide incentives for efficiency. Full hedging may well mean that an unexpected currency movement will result in a large loss for a manufacturing or sales division and a corresponding profit on the associated hedge by the treasury division of the company, or the converse. Incentivising parts of the business on the basis of recorded profits sits uncomfortably with a strategy of spreading risks across different parts of the business.

There is also a more fundamental reason why full hedging does not make sense. In practice, companies face many uncertainties: exchange-rate uncertainty is just one. Faced with multiple uncertainties, it does not pay a company to hedge fully against one particular risk, because that may leave it more exposed to other risks, so it is usually best to hedge only partially against any one risk. Only in the very special case where one can hedge against all risks simultaneously (which would require very complex forms of contract, which with good reason markets are usually unwilling to supply), would it make sense to hedge fully.

No such thing as a perfect hedge

Consider a specific example. Imagine a car company making a long-term investment in a factory in Germany, to supply the German, UK and D-mark currency-zone markets. (In reality, such a facility would supply other markets as well, but for simplicity put that to one side.) Such a long-term investment would be exposed to sustained movements in the £:DM exchange rate. A rise in the D-mark against sterling would make the factory less profitable, since it would be more difficult to sell at a profit into the UK market: by raising D-mark costs relative to sterling prices, it cuts either profit margins or sales. Symmetrically, a fall in the D-mark against sterling would improve the factory's profitability.

In principle, the company could assess its total currency exposure for the lifetime of the factory (looking forward five, ten or more years). This would involve, among other things, an assessment of sales into the future and their division between the two currencies. It could then hedge its overall currency risk. Since the swap market provides an efficient and cheap way of hedging, this is a feasible course of action. But it is not an attractive one. The future stream of profits from the factory is uncertain for a variety of reasons, including the strength of competition, both in terms of cost and product innovation, and the company's ability to supply, including productivity and wage trends. To hedge fully against the exchange-rate risk, but not the other risks, would be a mistake. True, it is feasible to lock into a particular exchange rate to hedge an anticipated stream of net earnings over the future, say for 20 years. But in plausible circumstances, this could result in commercial disaster.

Consider the effects of a sharp rise in UK wages relative to German wages. This is likely to lead, though perhaps not immediately, to a depreciation of sterling against the D-mark, so that relative wage costs, expressed in a common currency, stay roughly the same. Unhedged companies are therefore hedged, not in accounting or financial terms but in a real economic sense, against unexpected movements in general wage costs, by virtue of the fact that exchange rates tend to move over the long term to offset differentials in nominal wage costs. A company that chose to hedge overtly against movements in nominal exchange rates would leave itself massively exposed to short- to medium-term shifts in relative wage costs between Germany and the UK.

The implication is that it is not optimal for companies, both for internal management reasons and for external reasons, to hedge their exchange-rate exposure fully, even if they had the management capacity to do so (which in any case is unlikely in small- to medium-sized companies). Exchange-rate uncertainty therefore matters, despite the capacity to hedge cheaply. An increased volatility of exchange rates imposes an unavoidable cost on non-financial businesses operating across currency boundaries. By the same token, eliminating exchange risk gives those companies a benefit not otherwise available.

Manufacturers gain most

An important point to note is that companies with long-lived assets are the ones most subject to exchange-rate uncertainty. Traders and grocers are much less exposed. It is the manufacturing sector, with long-lived factories, that would benefit most from the elimination of exchange risk. Financial businesses, and the trading sector more generally, are also exposed through their investment in reputation, goodwill and personnel development. But their exposure tends on average to be less. This is true even when they trade in long-term assets, in which their positions are more easily liquidated. So they have less to gain from a single currency. And if EMU happens, the financial sector will lose part of its trade in currencies—of which more shortly.

The consequence of the euro for non-financial businesses would therefore be the removal of exchange-rate inhibitions on investment and cash-flow management in Europe. This would strengthen the European corporate finance function. Because of the increased competitiveness of the European equity market (see Chapter 7), companies may well enjoy the benefits of more competitive capital markets. It could also facilitate and motivate the rationalisation of treasury and corporate finance functions within companies that are diversified on a European scale, bringing further efficiency gains.

We can, therefore, expect the euro to bring in its train a radically reshaped treasury function and a more integrated market environment in Europe. This will act to the advantage of those companies that are competitive in Europe, and the disadvantage of those that are not.

Dangers: Eurosclerosis writ large

But a single currency is not without its dangers for business. The chief one is that the extra transparency brought by a single currency may lead to the "Europeanising" of labour markets across the EMU zone. This could lead to increased comparison of wages across the zone, particularly in sectors where trade unions wield bargaining power. If this led to a levelling up of wages, it could pose a major problem to companies operating in low wage economies, raising their wage costs and undermining their ability to compete. With the option of devaluation removed by the single currency, such extra labour-market rigidities would inflict major damage on weaker economies in Europe. The nightmare of a single currency is that it removes just those elements of labour-market flexibility that are required for adjustment in the absence of the option of exchange-rate realignments.

By contrast, comparisons that took relative efficiency as well as wages into account would be beneficial. With proper benchmarking of performance in one country against that in others, the consequence would be enhanced overall productivity. And if greater transparency also brought about improved labour mobility across the European market, this could help to increase labour supply, reducing national skill bottlenecks and enhancing the flexibility of the European labour market.

Jobs, wages and the social chapter

It is not obvious why companies should allow wage bargainers to impose the wage rigidities of the single currency nightmare. The issue of wage comparisons is a familiar one inside multinational companies operating across many countries. European MNCs are no exception. But such companies are well used to deploying the weapon of productivity comparisons to rebut unrealistic wage comparisons, and indeed this is often a good way to spur rationalisation and greater efficiency. This will not be altered by the introduction of a single currency. Other companies negotiate in a more national context. They too can deploy the weapon of efficiency comparisons across countries. But in any case, international wage comparisons can easily be dismissed since national labour markets are so weakly integrated.

If workers are unwilling to move from one country to another within the EMU zone, then arguments based on wage comparisons across countries are somewhat empty. Such relative wage comparisons would be relevant if labour were more willing to move; but if greater labour market flexibility resulted from EMU, far from being a threat, that would greatly enhance the operation of a single currency.

The most plausible way in which the nightmare could be realised is through greater and more harmonised regulation of Europe's labour markets through a strengthening and ossification of the EU's social chapter. Inflexible job tenure rights for workers, greater provision of poorly designed social benefits, inappropriate restrictions on wage setting and other measures could all act to increase the rigidity of the European labour market, particularly if applied across the EMU zone without regard for national circumstances. Of course, this could happen without EMU. But its consequences could be more serious in the absence of exchange-rate flexibility. The success of EMU, if it happens, depends on avoiding inappropriate regulation and harmonisation of European labour markets. As noted earlier, Europe faces a choice between, on one hand, a centralised and harmonised form of federation, and on the other, a decentralised federation in which subsidiarity is taken seriously. This is one aspect of that choice.

If EMU fails to work well, then this will impose a major cost on business. This takes us back to the macroeconomic arguments of Chapter 4. The primary risks identified there were: a more turbulent economic cycle because of the lack of national flexibility in monetary policy; higher unemployment and stagnation in some countries; more public debt and higher interest rates; and greater instability in the exchange rate of the euro against the dollar and yen. These are all possibilities, though as we also noted they are by no means inevitable. We return to these issues in the concluding chapter.

What business needs to do

Start preparing now

The euro will reduce by one the number of variables affecting business decisions, but at the cost, as some would see it, of greater macroeconomic policy rigour. Whatever their view of the pros and cons, firms will have to adapt to deal with a single currency in Europe if it happens. In particular, firms will need to address the following.

- **Prices and transactions technologies.** In the transition, companies may have to cope with dual pricing in euros and national currencies. This will put a strain on businesses, especially in retailing, which handle many small transactions. Cash tills, credit-card readers and accounting computer systems will all need to be adapted. The conversion will be most far-reaching for companies based in the EMU zone and with the bulk of their business there. But companies based outside the EMU zone with significant business within it will also need to consider how best to adapt. The scope for errors, with consequent loss of customer goodwill, is considerable.

- **Treasury function.** With appreciable change in European financial markets after the introduction of the euro (see Chapters 6 and 7), companies must adapt to take advantage. With greater competition, there may be savings in the cost of the treasury function to be derived from consolidating and/or shifting cash operations.

- **The denomination of debt and equity.** It will be mandatory for all companies to switch debt and equity denominated in participating currencies by early 2002, when national currencies disappear. But it may be beneficial to switch sooner to take early advantage of the deeper markets in euro securities that will be created. And companies may also wish to reconsider the currency denomination of their debt after the introduction of the euro. If European markets develop strongly, this may provide a good reason for issuing a larger proportion of euro-denominated securities.

- **Financial reporting.** Companies will need to consider the timing of the switch from reporting accounts in national currencies to reporting in the euro.

- **Taxes.** Some companies may find that the advent of the single currency changes their tax position. This might occur because of the conversion of an uncertain profit or loss into a certain one, crystallising the profit or loss for tax purposes. Thus, for example, a company holding a long-term interest swap in two participating currencies will know for certain the value of that swap, which may therefore affect its tax position.

This is a demanding agenda. Companies that fail to make adequate preparation may find themselves in difficulty if and when the euro is introduced, forcing them to devote an undue amount of management time to catching up. And it is a mistake for those companies that will be outside the EMU zone to assume that they need do nothing. If EMU works, and the euro becomes attractive, "out" companies will need to think about how their competition may turn the euro to advantage. Early consideration of these issues will yield a pay-off.

Chapter 6 EMU and the banks

Profound changes lie ahead

In this chapter we examine the consequences of EMU for the banking sector. Our aim is not to provide a manual for experts working in the sector, but rather to give insights for the non-specialist. For banks and other operators in the markets for short-term money and foreign exchange, currency is the raw material of the business. For such firms, adopting the euro represents a profound change in the business environment. Business strategies and practices will need to change accordingly.

Main effects of EMU on European banking

Whole sector

- Increased competition across national borders in EMU zone, both on price and service quality.
- Rationalisation of banking structure, with more pan-European players together with niche banks.
- Elimination of foreign-exchange trading in European currencies participating in EMU.
- Growing importance of euro banking business as euro becomes increasingly important for trade both in Europe and in the wider international economy.

Insider banks

- Suffer from the use of reserve requirements, representing a tax on banking business, in the ECB's conduct of monetary policy.
- Benefit from access to the TARGET system for real-time gross euro settlements.
- Suffer disproportionately relative to some outsider banks from the loss of intra-EMU foreign exchange dealings.
- Risk inadequate preparation for euro clearing, particularly in those countries where participation in EMU is unclear.
- Incur significant extra costs.

Outsider banks

- Benefit from lack of reserve requirements imposed by the ECB.
- Suffer limited access to TARGET, with possible consequent extra cost in euro transactions.
- Carry the extra cost of maintaining dual clearing systems and reserves for both euro and domestic business.
- Risk inadequate preparation for euro clearing, and may therefore be at a competitive disadvantage in a growing market.

Thorough preparation is needed

The most obvious adaptation that banks in the EMU zone will have to make is to convert their operations from individual national currencies to euros. In the transition to EMU, this will require a thorough overhaul of banks' systems and operating procedures. This is a major task, for which a number of leading banks in those countries most likely to participate (France and Germany in particular) have already started intense preparations.

Accounts, standing orders and other arrangements will all need to be converted. Although this is a straightforward arithmetic operation, the scale of the conversion means that there is ample scope for error. Bank machines (ATMs) will have to be converted to handle euros rather than national notes. Fortunately, the technology is such that conversion is generally feasible, avoiding the need to replace the machines. The scope for confusion when national currencies are withdrawn and replaced by the euro is great. To avoid errors in clearing cheques, for example, effective and efficient procedures will be needed to distinguish between cheques drawn in euros and those drawn in national currencies. Banks will be concerned to make the transition as smooth as possible, to avoid impairing their reputation for efficiency and customer service. Employees will require training throughout the organisation, from counter staff to senior managers. Matters are made still more difficult because at the same time the banks (and other organisations) will be grappling with the computer software problems associated with the turn of the year 2000.

The banks will need to ensure that their euro payments and clearing systems are up and running, a task which rests largely with the clearing houses responsible for these functions. There is also the Ecu Banking Association, which plans to convert its current ecu clearing system to euros and to expand it fiftyfold to meet the demand for euro clearing; since the ecu will convert to the euro on a one-to-one basis, such a system could become a key part of international euro dealings. However, individual banks will also need to modify the computer software that provides the gateways to these systems. The international competitive position of national banks will depend in part on the efficiency of the euro clearing systems to which they are linked. Weaknesses in these could well cause business to be lost to countries with well-functioning payments systems.

Intensifying competition

In addition to these issues of logistics, it seems likely that banking within the euro area will become the arena for much stronger competitive pressures. In ordinary commercial banking, the presence of many currencies has acted like a barrier to competition: a bank wishing to enter the market of another member country needed to establish systems allowing it to operate in the other national currency, and this raised the costs of entry. More generally, European banking has been very balkanised, with severe limits on crossborder competition.

By removing this barrier to entry, EMU will strengthen competitive pressures among the various national banking systems. In effect, it will reinforce the various banking directives associated with the single market, which have already helped to remove other barriers to crossborder competition between banks in the EU. So far, the single market has had disappointing results in this industry, largely because the second banking directive, which was agreed to in 1992, has only recently come into force.

In the short term, a fiercer level of competition will lead to competitive incursions by banks across national borders into markets previously dominated by domestic banks. Such incursions will be into the more profitable parts of the markets, and with lower-cost technology than that of the incumbent firms.

For example, new entrants may offer telephone banking to avoid the need to build up a branch banking network, and target the most profitable segment of the customer base. There is considerable scope for this in the mortgage and consumer credit markets across Europe. Entry of this kind will put considerable pressure on incumbents saddled with an expensive branch network, which is difficult to divest. By cherry-picking the most profitable segments of the market, such entry will also act to unwind the cross-subsidies that are characteristic of traditional banking. This new competition will lead to cheaper and better services for the customers who have paid for the cross-subsidies in the past, but could produce higher prices and deteriorating services for those who formerly benefited.

In the medium to longer run, stronger competition is likely to lead to a restructuring of the European banking system. Efficient banks will expand in the euro zone, both by organic growth and by mergers and takeovers; inefficient ones will reduce their activities or be taken over.

Exposed nerves

All this is bound to offend national sensitivities. If, for example, a major national bank faces being taken over by a bank from another country, there will be calls for rationalisation to be checked. This could well delay the emergence of a more efficient banking system in Europe. The pressures will be much the same as the ones encountered earlier in Europe's industrial sectors. (Recall how the disappearance of the last big UK-owned car company raised such concerns in the UK.) Incumbent managers and workers will undoubtedly claim that banks are different, in an effort to protect their vested interests. Ultimately, however, market forces and commercial logic will force rationalisation, as in other industries.

The result is likely to be fewer commercial banks in Europe and the emergence of pan-EMU banking. Some banks will provide general services and others will operate in niche markets, but in either case operations are likely to extend across the EMU zone. Purely national banks may continue, but to survive they will need to become more efficient and position themselves more carefully. This rationalised system will deliver a cheaper and better service with wider choice: the customer will be the ultimate beneficiary. But a likely side-effect will be job losses in traditional labour-intensive branch banking. Again, EMU will deliver in banking some of the benefits that the single market programme has delivered in other sectors of European industry: a greater scale of operation, leading to economies of scale, and stronger competition, lowering prices and improving customer choice. Some banks will disappear or be taken over, but those that remain will be better placed to compete internationally. The evidence is that a strongly competitive market at home helps firms to compete internationally. This is as true of banking as of other businesses.

The euro settlement system

TARGET

A competitive euro banking system will require an integrated and efficient settlements system. The preparations for EMU include plans by the EMI for the so-called TARGET (Trans-European Automated Real-Time Gross Settlement Express Transfer) system. This will link the national clearing systems of EMU members.

In the past, clearing between banks has traditionally taken place at the end of the day, with settlements between the banks reflecting the net positions arrived at as a result of an enormous number of gross transactions. But settling at the end of the day introduces a risk: if the settlement system is not instantaneous, there will be many unsettled transactions between banks at any point in time. If a bank collapses, other banks with claims on it will suffer losses: in this way, bank failure can spread. Even if net claims between any two banks balance, there is still an exposure. The claims of a failed bank on any other are enforceable by the receivers of the failed bank: healthy banks may have to pay their obligations in full, while receiving only part-payment, and after considerable delay, as creditors of the failed bank. The growing practice of "netting" (a legal device to make the bank liable only for its net position to a defaulting bank) helps to reduce this problem, but substantial exposures can still remain.

The need to eliminate these risks, and to achieve other efficiencies, has motivated a general move to real-time gross settlement (RTGS) systems. These have been made possible by the rapid advance in computing and communications technology. Each transaction between banks is settled immediately, rather than on a net basis at the end of the day. Some residual exposure remains: even with modern technology, settlements cannot be absolutely instantaneous. (The German RTGS system currently settles every half hour.) Also, these systems greatly increase the banks' needs for liquidity, because the balance of transactions within the day is much more volatile than the balance at the end of the day. This has implications for the operation of EMU.

Reserve requirements in EMU

One important competitive disadvantage for banks operating within the EMU zone is likely to be minimum reserve requirements. These have been a traditional tool of monetary control: the central bank requires banks to hold a certain proportion of their deposits in specified liquid reserves, often deposits at the central bank or short-term government paper.

The need for such reserves is sometimes argued on prudential grounds: they strengthen banks against runs and other market pressures such as bad loans. Alternatively, they may be justified in terms of monetary policy: minimum reserves make it easier for the central bank to influence bank deposits (ie, the supply of broad money). Both arguments are disputed. Liquidity against bank runs need not take the form of government paper or deposits with the central bank. And monetary policy works mainly through the effects of the central bank's money-market operations on interest rates; arguably, bank reserves have little influence on this.

The central banks themselves disagree about the need for reserve requirements. The Bank of England dispensed with them altogether in the 1980s. By contrast, the Bundesbank argues that they are important for the conduct of its monetary policy. A crucial argument in the EMI, and in future in the ECB, centres on whether the ECB should deploy reserve requirements as part of its armoury of monetary policy weapons. Since the Bundesbank is a dominant influence on EMI and likely ECB thinking, it seems probable that reserve requirements will be used, though at what level and on what terms remains open.

A tax on banks

Reserve requirements act, in effect, as a tax on the banks. If reserves have to be held in the form of non-interest bearing deposits with the central bank, then the bank must earn a higher return on the rest of its assets, which in turn implies higher loan rates. If other financial institutions (either non-banks or banks outside the EMU zone) are free from this "tax", they will win business from the more controlled banking sector. This was the experience in the UK in the 1960s and 1970s, when the uncontrolled non-bank financial intermediary sector grew much faster than the controlled banking sector. The same point applies, though with less force, if reserves have to be held in short-term government paper. By artificially increasing the demand for such paper, the rules raise its price and lower its rate of return. The taxation element is lower than in the case of non-interest bearing deposits, because some interest is received, but the rules still weaken the competitive position of the banks on which they are imposed.

Foreign-exchange operations

EMU will also influence the foreign-exchange operations of banks. It will eliminate altogether the transactions that currently take place between the currencies of the countries participating in EMU. How large a volume of transactions this will be depends on the number of countries participating.

In addition, EMU will shift the pattern of other foreign-exchange dealings. It seems possible that the euro will be more widely adopted than the existing national currencies for invoicing and transactions purposes in international trade with non-EMU countries. If most EU countries participate in EMU, and if EMU monetary policy makes the euro a stable currency, then the euro may well become more attractive as a vehicle currency in world trade, taking some of the trade currently conducted in dollars. Today, for instance, most trade between Asia and Europe is conducted in dollars, not in European currencies. The euro could change this. Many potential users, especially in Asia, will doubtless be cautious, preferring to wait until the euro has established its credentials as a sound currency. Even if all goes well, a decade or more may pass before the euro displaces the dollar to any significant extent.

In its effects on the foreign-exchange operations of banks operating within EMU, therefore, the euro is pulling in two different directions. On the one hand, the abolition of trade in some European currencies will remove a significant part of their business. (This will matter more to banks in Paris and Frankfurt than to those in London, which have a more diversified forex business.) On the other hand, euro trading could prove a fast growing business.

(Taking this into account, London especially could be a net beneficiary.) As we note later, EMU is also likely to stimulate growth in the fixed-interest markets, from which banks could benefit further.

Beyond the euro zone

Will EMU-based banks be better placed than non-EMU ones to take this business? Banks outside EMU, particularly those operating from European countries that remain outside, whether by choice or necessity, need to consider whether exclusion from EMU will place them at a competitive disadvantage; or whether on the contrary, as some argue, exclusion will bring competitive opportunities. The issue is especially important for countries where banking is a big business, notably Switzerland and the UK. Switzerland cannot participate in EMU because it is not in the EU. The UK has an opt-out from EMU which it is likely to exercise when the time comes, regardless of whether a Conservative or a Labour government is in power.

A key question for non-EMU banks is whether they will be able to take part in the system of euro-clearing, since this provides the basis for an efficient payments system. As described above, the EMI is currently planning TARGET, a euro-clearing system that will link the RTGS networks of each of the banking systems participating in EMU. Non-EMU RTGS systems will also be linked to TARGET to facilitate international transactions. The important issue is not the fact of connection, but the terms. What matters to banks outside the EMU zone is whether they can access TARGET on attractive terms. If not, banks outside EMU may find it more difficult to compete effectively for euro-denominated business, which if EMU is a success could be the fastest growing part of the banking market.

Access to TARGET, on what terms?

The terms of access to TARGET are ultimately for the ECB to determine. A cause for concern is that only those countries participating within EMU will be represented on the ECB. The suspicion is that the terms will be manipulated in order to advance the interests of the banks of participating countries, to the disadvantage of the others.

The single-market directives should act as a check on this. The various banking directives aim to create a level playing field for banking across the whole of the EU, not just within EMU. Overt discrimination against outsiders could fall foul of these rules, and be struck down by the European Court. But this is uncertain. In addition, the directives allow exceptions to the principle of a level playing-field, if these can be shown to be needed for the conduct of the common monetary policy.

Moreover, there are good reasons why access to TARGET by outsiders might be on poorer terms. A crucial issue is access to euro liquidity provided by the ECB as lender of last resort. Central banks around the world provide liquidity to their banking and money markets to ensure their smooth operation. Normally, banks that find themselves short of liquidity can borrow short-term from the central bank. The central bank may also intervene to aid banks that are in deeper financial difficulty: a bank that is solvent but loses the confidence of its customers may survive with central bank guarantees or go under without them. The central-bank functions of prudential supervision, providing liquidity and acting as lender of last resort are difficult in practice to separate; different central banks choose their own emphasis. Some, notably the Bundesbank, have limited their role to providing liquidity, not rescuing insolvent banks. But others at various times have acted to help ailing banks, which runs the risk of undermining responsible monetary policy.

The ECB: whose lender of last resort?

Within the proposed EMU zone, the ECB will act as lender of last resort. It is very likely to model itself on the Bundesbank, limiting its role to the provision of short-term liquidity where necessary, and always subject to the sound conduct of monetary policy. An important question for banks operating outside the EMU zone is whether, and on what terms, they will have access to the ECB for euro liquidity.

The ECB's role clearly demands that it provide euro liquidity to banks within the EMU zone, but it is far from clear why it should be expected to do the same for banks outside. Thus the Bank of England supplies sterling liquidity to banks operating in the UK, but not to support the sterling operations of banks outside the UK, and the same is true of other central banks around the world. Indeed, were it to do so, the sterling operations of banks outside the UK could well influence the conduct of UK monetary policy and interfere with its effectiveness.

It seems probable that outsider banks will not have access to TARGET on terms identical to those of insider banks. The appropriate question will be how restricted their access should be. It is also clear that, in determining the terms of access, the key criterion should be to maximise access (in accordance with the terms of the single market) subject to the ECB retaining full control over the conduct of euro monetary policy.

Access to intra-day liquidity from the ECB is of crucial importance to outsider banks. Without it they will be forced to hold very large reserves of euro liquidity themselves to provide for the large intra-day swings in settlements that are possible with RTGS. This would place them at a clear competitive disadvantage to insider banks, for which access to ECB liquidity would reduce the need to hold euro reserves. Arguably, such access by outsider banks to intra-day euro liquidity from the ECB would not seriously weaken the ECB's power over monetary policy, since hour-to-hour movements in liquidity are of limited significance for monetary policy. However, the counter-argument, advanced especially in France and Germany, is that access to intra-day liquidity needs to be limited because of the risk that intra-day borrowings can spill over into overnight settlements. Thus it is argued that outsider banks should be granted very restricted access to euro liquidity towards the end of the trading day, so as to ensure that intra-day transactions do not spill over into an overnight position.

It has always been clear that France and Germany would deny outsider banks access to overnight euro liquidity. However, at one stage in 1996 it seemed possible that a deal would be struck to allow outsiders intra-day access. That now seems less likely, though the final decision will be taken by the ECB. The implication is that, without alternative arrangements for access to euro liquidity, outsider banks will be at a competitive disadvantage. Whereas an insider bank will be able to go to the ECB for euro liquidity to meet a short intra-day or overnight settlements position, outsider banks will not, and without alternative arrangements will therefore need to hold larger euro reserves against this contingency.

Options for outsiders

Fortunately, there are several ways that outsider banks can get access to euro liquidity even without direct access to TARGET. They could establish a branch in the EMU zone, for example in Frankfurt or Paris, and use that branch's access to TARGET to clear their euro business; in effect, the branch inside the euro zone makes them an insider bank. Although there have been rumours that participating members might restrict access to TARGET through this route, this would seem to be a clear contravention of single-market rules and would presumably be struck down by the European Court. Alternatively, they may make use of a correspondent bank arrangement: the traditional way of clearing foreign-exchange dealings by arrangement through another bank. Currently, arrangements through correspondent banks are uneconomic, but if the volume of such business grows considerably, as it would if London banks were outside EMU and used such arrangements to settle their euro business, it could become much more attractive. And other clearing systems, such as the enhanced version of that provided by the Ecu Banking Association, could provide other options.

Less advantageous access to TARGET need not strike a major blow to outsider banks. If it does have an impact, it may be more likely to shift banking activity towards insider countries as banks adapt the geographical balance of their activity, rather than putting individual banks directly at a disadvantage.

EMU's competitive threat to outsider banks

Even without limits on their use of TARGET, outsider banks could find themselves at a commercial disadvantage in euro business because they are required to maintain a domestic currency business alongside their euro business. The need to maintain a dual system and be concerned about liquidity in two currencies (the home currency and the euro) will require some duplication of functions. Outsider banks are likely to find it easy to hold on to their domestic currency activity, but may need to be that much more efficient to compete effectively for euro banking business.

A factor working in the other direction, to the advantage of outsider banks, would be the imposition of significant reserve requirements on insider banks, in the form of deposits yielding zero or below-market rates of interest. These would operate, as noted above, like a tax on insider banks, and could outweigh many times any disadvantage arising from more limited access to TARGET. However, policy-makers at the EMI are well aware of this, and it seems likely that any reserve requirements imposed by the ECB will be set low, and will call for deposits paying interest close to market rates. It is probably unwise for prospective outsider banks to rely on this as a source of competitive advantage if EMU goes ahead.

A further issue is the impact of EMU on bank business in foreign exchange. We have already noted that the abolition of those currencies participating in EMU will eliminate part of this business. Intra-EMU transactions, which will disappear, account for a large proportion of the foreign-exchange business of those banks (notably French and German) likely to participate in EMU, and a relatively small proportion of the business of those banks (notably British and Swiss) that could well be outside. If these insider banks find it hard to adjust to the loss of this business, this could put them at a competitive disadvantage vis-à-vis outsider banks in London or Zurich. An important lesson of business strategy is that adverse shocks that hit your competitor more severely than you can provide a business opportunity. The restructuring of foreign exchange dealings with the advent of EMU might be one such shock.

Be prepared!

An efficient euro payment system is a key factor in the competitive position of the banking system. In this, there is likely to be a first-mover advantage: banks that can offer early on an efficient, cost-effective euro payments service will secure an appreciable share of this expanding market. In order to do so, such banks, either individually or more likely in collaboration with others, must put in place the payments and clearing infrastructure to facilitate this, which requires up-front investment. Ambivalence and uncertainty about UK participation in EMU may make this difficult. In countries such as France, where the commitment to participation is far stronger, banks have more reason to plan and commit resources. British banks need to be making preparations for a euro clearing system whether or not the UK participates in EMU, if they are not to lose out to continental competitors. If such preparations are not made in time, British banks could be placed at a significant disadvantage in euro banking.

Electronic money

An important innovation in banking is electronic money: smart cards, containing computer microchips, that act as money. These will be used rather like generalised phone cards, to pay retailers for goods and services; and they will be rechargeable by being plugged into a bank cash dispenser or telephone.

This is a hotly contested market, with all the major global credit and charge-card organisations, such as Visa, Mastercard and Europay, holding trials. Mondex, a UK-led global consortium of 17 banks, has been testing a system in Britain for more than a year. Some of these cards are incompatible with other card systems, requiring retailers to maintain multiple point-of-sale terminals. NTT, the Japanese telecoms giant, is developing a card that is compatible with other credit and charge-card systems and thereby avoids this problem.

The electronic money market will grow rapidly whether or not EMU happens. Its relevance to EMU is that smart money can cope with a multi-currency world, and therefore the switch to the euro, with ease. EMU greatly enhances the attractiveness of electronic money as a way of coping with the transitional problems of 1999-2002, when retailers will need to handle both national and euro transactions. But electronic cash also has implications for the benefits of EMU. If smart money overcomes many of the conversion problems of conventional notes and coin, then it also removes one of the (admittedly minor) reasons for moving to the euro.

Chapter 7 EMU and the capital markets

EMU raises important issues for the development and operation of securities markets in Europe. In this chapter, we examine some of the key issues, to give a view of how financial markets will develop as a consequence of EMU. As in the previous chapter, our aim is to provide an overview of the key issues for the non-specialist, not to provide a comprehensive analysis for the specialist financial-market insider. We consider first the issues raised by the transition; and then move on to the longer-run consequences for asset management and securities markets.

The continuity of financial contracts

Will debts be honoured?

If EMU occurs, it is important that the actual transition from individual European currencies to the euro does not represent a major disruption to financial markets. In particular, it is crucial that long-term contracts entered into before EMU that last beyond the introduction of the euro should be appropriately honoured. This is not automatic: a contract struck in Dutch guilders, for example, will have to be honoured after EMU by payment in euros, and one or other of the parties to the contract might argue that this was inappropriate.

If circumstances allowed such contracts to be cancelled, the consequences would be profound. Companies (or even governments) that had borrowed long-term at high interest rates in the past could take the opportunity to repay such debt at face value and issue new debt at lower interest rates, thereby easing their debt burden. The pension, insurance and other funds that had invested in the original debt in good faith would suffer a substantial capital loss, to the detriment of their beneficiaries. Even a small possibility that long-term contracts would not continue would cause major disruption in financial markets: since very large sums of money are potentially involved, there is a strong incentive for legal challenges to such contracts to be mounted, even with a quite low probability of success. Since the legal process works slowly, the uncertainty and confusion caused by such challenges, if they occurred, would be considerable.

In many respects, this is an old and familiar legal problem, since currency reforms have happened frequently in history. The new French franc replaced the old one in 1960; the last two zeros were deleted from the old money. Similar reforms in Latin American countries have been common to deal with the problem of rapid inflation. Among major currencies, only the dollar and sterling have been immune to such reforms, reflecting the generally low historical levels of inflation in the USA and the UK over the past century. Law around the world has therefore had to devise rules for handling such changes.

The importance of *Lex Monetae*

The so-called *Lex Monetae*, recognised generally around the world, prescribes that, in the event of a currency reform legislated by government, changing an old currency into a new one at a specified conversion rate, the currency denomination of existing contracts will be converted to the new currency at the specified rate without alteration of other aspects of the contract. Thus a government owing money to holders of bonds denominated in the national currency, for example, is entitled to repay the principal in the new currency, at the specified conversion rate. The same is true of the interest: the rate of interest paid on the bonds remains the same, irrespective of whether the new currency turns out to be "hard" or "soft". *Lex Monetae* means that the legal defence of "frustration", that external circumstances beyond the control of the contractee prevent completion of the contract, will not be available to those in default of such contracts. On this basis, existing D-mark contracts will be enforceable in euros. Moreover, given the general recognition of this principle in legal systems around the world, D-mark contracts written on Wall Street between non- Germans would be enforceable in the New York courts. Thus continuity of contracts in national currencies is not a problem.

However, *Lex Monetae* applies only to currencies and does not apply to ecu contracts, because the ecu is a basket of 12 European currencies, not a currency in its own right. (It should be noted that the definition of the ecu has not been expanded to incorporate the currencies of the three recent new EU members, Austria, Finland, and Sweden.) An issue therefore arises over the continuity of ecu contracts. Since the ecu bond market is large, this is a cause for concern. However, following representations from the banking and securities industry, particularly from London, the December 1996 Dublin summit agreed that EU countries will introduce legislation ahead of the transition to a single currency that specifies the conversion of the ecu and therefore avoids the possible discontinuity of contracts, and the consequent disruption to financial markets.

It also seems likely, though not guaranteed, that other jurisdictions, such as New York State, will take the lead from European law, provided this lead is sufficiently clear. (One complication is that any decision at a US state level may be appealed against at the federal level.) The issue of continuity of contract need not prove troublesome, if it is properly addressed in advance.

What becomes of the ecu?

However, a question remains over the conversion of the ecu into the euro. The Maastricht treaty assumes that the ecu will be converted into the euro at one-to-one. This was confirmed by the Madrid summit in December 1995. It would pose no difficulty if all 12 of the constituent currencies making up the ecu were to participate in EMU: the euro would simply replace the ecu in all 12 countries. But matters are more complicated with a partial EMU, which indeed is likely to involve at least one member state (Austria) whose currency is not included in the ecu. In this case, making the ecu convertible into the euro at one-to-one will generate inequities and other problems.

To see this, consider a very simplified EU divided into two: the "ins" with hard currencies and the "outs" with soft currencies. (This is over simple because the currencies of the voluntary "outs", such as the UK, may also be hard, but the simplification helps to illustrate the essential point.) Suppose that the "ins" account for two-thirds of the ecu basket, the "outs" accounting for the remaining third. Suppose that the "ins" have an average interest rate of 7%, and the "outs" an average interest rate of 10%. This interest differential of 3% reflects the market expectation, ahead of EMU, that the softer "out" currencies will depreciate on average by 3% per year against the "in" currencies.

Now consider in this example the effect of converting the ecu into the euro on a one-to-one basis. Prior to conversion, the ecu interest rate was 8% (two-thirds of the "ins" interest rate of 7% and one-third of the "outs" interest rate of 10%), reflecting the basket composition of the ecu. With conversion, the interest rate falls to 7%. Before conversion, the ecu was expected to depreciate on average 1% per year against the "in" currencies and appreciate 2% against the "outs". With conversion, the ecu becomes the "in" currency (the euro) and is expected to appreciate 3% on average against the "out" currencies.

So it makes a material difference to the holders of ecus whether EMU proceeds. With EMU, the ecu becomes a harder currency than without EMU, and contracts written in ecus are, in effect, rewritten in a stronger currency. The consequences are profound. Long-dated ecu securities will be worth more if EMU proceeds than if it does not. Some of this effect will be in the current price, since markets have already incorporated expectations of EMU occurring into their valuation. But as EMU becomes a more certain prospect, some further capital gain can be expected. If, however, EMU is derailed, then capital losses will occur.

On the other side, those who have borrowed long-term in ecus will find that the cost of servicing that debt is increased by EMU. Thus the interest payments, in effect, have to be paid in a harder currency than anticipated, rather as though a debt in Italian lire was converted into D-marks. Long-term ecu borrowers could argue that, in effect, they have had their contract rewritten to their detriment: having initially contracted to pay a higher interest rate to reflect the relative softness of the ecu, they find the ecu transformed into a hard currency without any re-contracting of the interest rate.

Soft currencies

From the economic perspective, the same issue applies to contracts in soft currencies, such as the lira. But the legal principle of *Lex Monetae* means that long-term contracts in lire must be honoured in euros, if Italy joins EMU; whereas the same legal principle does not extend to the ecu. Thus *Lex Monetae* creates a potentially sharp divide between ecu and soft-currency contracts.

It is possible that this implicit redefinition of the ecu with EMU could provide the basis for an effective legal challenge to the continuity of long-term ecu contracts. If European legal safeguards against this are put in place, such a challenge could be mounted outside European jurisdictions, for example in New York or Japan. This may be unlikely, but if it did occur it would cause some disturbance in ecu bond markets. It seems that one-to-one conversion of the ecu was insufficiently examined by European policy-makers. The drafters of the Maastricht treaty thought too little about the consequences of a partial EMU, with "ins" and "outs". Fuller consideration might well have led to the alternative of maintaining the ecu as a basket currency, with the existing currencies that do not participate in EMU in the basket alongside the euro. This arrangement would have avoided the problems of continuity. It would also have avoided the associated difficulty of pre-announcing the EMU parities to avoid the risk of currency speculation in Phase 3B, as discussed in Chapter 3. But an objection to this alternative is that ecu bond issues over the past few years have been based on the expectation of a one-to-one conversion; arguably, this possibility and the associated uncertainties should have been taken into account by those entering into ecu contracts after Maastricht. Changing course at this stage would introduce a new discontinuity into such contracts.

An awkward truth: no way out

The truth is that there was no way of avoiding a discontinuity in ecu contracts: the one-to-one conversion enshrined in Maastricht introduces a change in long-term ecu contracts entered into before EMU became a possibility, while a shift from this would introduce a change in contracts entered into afterwards. What is clear is that, with the adoption of one-to-one conversion, there is a sounder basis for challenges through the courts to ecu contracts entered into before Maastricht, when the principle of one-to-one conversion was enshrined, than to ecu contracts entered into afterwards, when contractors should have been aware of this likelihood. The European Commission has responded by drafting legislation to avoid legal challenges to existing contracts. Given the enormous sums that might be secured by a successful challenge, the possibility of a challenge cannot be ruled out.

Other transitional issues

The securities markets will have to confront a host of other technical matters. Some are issues for individual businesses, some require coordination among different businesses, and others may require government action.

Converting debt to euros

The strength and efficiency of securities markets depend on the volume of trading. High levels of transactions make sales easy to effect, and therefore give liquidity to securities. If securities can readily be disposed of by investors, then this in turn augments the attraction of holding such securities, adding in turn to the efficiency of the market. Whether the euro is to become an important currency not just in transactions but also in securities markets may therefore depend on whether a large volume of securities trading in euros becomes established at an early stage.

Three main factors will determine the growth of euro securities markets:

- the volume of new issues of euro securities (ie, the strength of the primary market in euro securities);
- the speed and extent of conversion of the existing stock of securities denominated in national currencies; and
- the conversion of the existing ecu market into euros.

The Maastricht treaty requires that the governments of those member states participating in EMU will issue euro debt from January 1, 1999, when national currencies are locked against each other but continue to circulate. This means that issues of government debt will be an important contributor to the growth of the euro fixed-interest debt market. But a strict application of the stability and growth pact will mean an average government debt issue of at most 3% of GDP. Since the average level of debt for participating countries is likely to be around 60-70% of GDP, new issues are likely to account at most for growth in the market of only 5% in nominal terms, or around 2.5-3% in real terms.

Since new primary issues are generally small in relation to the outstanding stock of securities, the dominant factor, certainly in the early years, may well prove to be the transfer of securities from national currency denomination into euros. The same point applies to private-sector debt. In the longer term, primary issues of private debt will determine the strength of the euro market, but in the transition to EMU the major influence will be the transfer of existing secondary national debt into euros.

Several governments committed to EMU have decided on a rapid conversion of existing national government debt into euro-denominated debts: thus the French and Belgian governments have decided to convert government debt into euros early in 1999, while the Germans are seriously considering that possibility. If this happens, it will quickly create a market in euro government debt, helping to establish deep markets in euro-denominated securities.

Companies with securities denominated in currencies participating in EMU will have to convert the denomination of their debt at the latest by early in 2002, when national currencies are to be withdrawn. But they have the option of earlier conversion from January 1, 1999. A number of governments are actively encouraging their companies to convert debt early. The advantage of this for the workings of EMU is the same: that it will quickly establish a large, efficient and liquid market in euro-denominated debt, both private and public.

Non-participants

The position will, of course, be different for those countries not participating in EMU. There is obviously no requirement for such countries to issue government debt in euros, and although it may from time to time make sense for such governments to issue euro-denominated debt, just as some have issued ecu debt in the past, this is unlikely to be the norm. Similarly, companies in these countries are unlikely to alter the denomination of the bulk of their debt from their national currencies. It is only for those minority of companies headquartered in an "out" but doing a large part of their business in the "ins" that it might make sense to switch debt, equity and reporting of company accounts into euros. For companies that operate worldwide, in Asia and the Americas as well as in Europe, the benefits of switching to the euro are also uncertain.

Forward planning of these matters is relatively easy for companies and governments in countries which are clearly either "in" or "out". For those countries where participation in EMU is possible but uncertain, either because the country may not meet the Maastricht convergence criteria or because of choice, forward planning must take the form of contingency planning, preparing for alternative scenarios until matters become clearer in early 1998.

The upshot is that securities issued by companies and governments of the countries participating in EMU will provide the staple business of the new euro securities markets. There will also be significant business from hedging and other financial operations by businesses operating internationally, but such business will arise from all parts of the world, including the USA and Japan, and not particularly from the European "outs".

Can the City of London succeed if the UK is out?

This raises an important question. Given that the governments and companies of the "in" countries will provide the staple of the new euro securities market, will this trade be concentrated in the "in" countries—say in Frankfurt or Paris? The realities of modern securities trading means that there is no inevitability about this. If London prepares properly for trading euro securities, there is no reason why it cannot take a large part of the market, even if the UK stays outside EMU. Exchange-based trade is highly mobile, moving to the most efficient low-cost exchange. London accounts for around 40% of foreign exchange dealings in the dollar and 50% of trade in German Bunds. As these examples show, lack of access to a euro settlement system need not prevent such trade flowing through London. The key will be the efficiency of London relative to other financial centres in Europe and elsewhere. In this, London has many advantages provided that it prepares well. But it needs to be aware that, stimulated by the prospect of EMU, European competition is hotting up. Frankfurt and Paris are both raising their game to compete for the new euro business, and London needs to respond effectively if it is not to lose out.

How to prepare

Securities firms need to do a variety of things. There is a need to prepare the various securities settlement systems for operating in euros. In the transition, this will mean dual systems to handle both euro and national currency trading. The need for dual systems will persist for the "outs" if they wish to compete effectively for euro business.

There may be a need to coordinate the re-denomination of debt, which raises a number of awkward technical issues. Markets prefer to trade in round units. The simple conversion of round units of national debt into euros will create debt with strings of decimal places for its value. There is therefore a need to re-parcel this debt into manageable units, preferably the same across all categories of debt to facilitate trade; and to resolve the problems of any awkward remainders that may be left over. The problem of the remainder might be dealt with by a cash repayment, or new issues to make up the total to a round number in euros. The different options suggest the need for some coordination between investors and issuers and possibly some overall market guidance.

If the aim is to create a deep and integrated euro market, then some harmonisation of other technical features across European markets will be required. Interest, for example, is calculated in different ways in different markets. Whereas UK, US and Japanese markets calculate interest on the basis of actual days elapsed and a 365-day year, other conventions abound in Europe. One convention uses a notional 360-day year divided into 30-day months, while another again adopts a 360-day year, but counts actual days.

Varying bank holidays in Europe are another problem. Practices on interest-rate fixing also vary, with some markets having same-day settlement after fixing and others operating with a two-day delay. It can be argued that this harmonisation is as much part of the single-market process in the EU as of the EMU process. But eliminating currency differences in financial contracts will highlight these inconsistencies and makes the need to eliminate them more pressing. Trading across European financial markets will be easier, the fewer the differences in market conventions.

The move to a single currency will reduce the range of financial market securities on offer. Whereas the same instrument written in francs and D-marks currently differs because of the currency risk on the franc:D-mark exchange rate, the introduction of the euro will make them the same instrument. In certain cases, this will have tax consequences, since the elimination of currency risk may convert a hitherto risky income stream into a certain one, which then under standard accounting conventions "crystallises" a capital gain or loss for tax purposes. Thus a fixed interest rate swap between two "in" currencies (say, the franc and D-mark) would convert into an annuity. Similar considerations apply to a foreign exchange option involving two "in" currencies.

EMU and investment behaviour

In many respects, the introduction of the euro will be a minor ripple for the investment management industry, for Europe's "ins" and "outs" and for the rest of the world. The world of investment management handles multiple currencies and the associated currency risk as a matter of routine. This is as true for those funds that take open positions on currencies, speculating on future movements, as it is for those funds that routinely hedge any currency exposure. It is true that some European currencies will disappear, and be replaced by the euro; and that some associated securities and derivatives denominated in these currencies will merge to become the same investment instruments in the absence of intra-EMU currency changes. But all this will represent a largely trivial change to the way that investment managers conduct their business.

However, the introduction of the euro in a significant number of EU countries will not be without implications for the investment environment internationally. EMU may help to remove some existing barriers to crossborder investment in Europe. EMU will alter the mix of available currencies, and therefore the characteristics of portfolios designed to hedge foreign-exchange risk. And if the ECB, by modelling itself on the Bundesbank, is able to ensure that the euro is a stable and strong currency, then the euro could establish itself as an important vehicle in international trade, altering the international demand for dollars and yen. These possible effects are rather uncertain, and it is therefore not easy to be definitive about them, either in terms of size or even direction.

Home bias because investors prefer it

The removal of crossborder barriers to investment could come through two main routes. First, many investment funds for sensible reasons care about the foreign exchange composition of their investments relative to their liabilities, and betray a domestic-currency or home bias. This need not imply a policy of matching the currency composition of their investments with those of their liabilities; but it does mean that funds care about foreign-exchange exposure. They therefore accept such exposure only if the likely return from doing so warrants the additional element of risk, or if a more diversified currency portfolio reduces overall risk: in an inflation-prone economy, for example, international diversification can therefore guard against losses from inflation—and consequent currency depreciation—at home.

Thus a German pension fund or insurance company has the great bulk of its liabilities in D-marks, in the form of pension rights and potential life or other insurance claims. It therefore makes sense for such institutions to invest the bulk of their funds in D-mark assets. Investments in other currencies leave the fund exposed to unforeseen appreciation of the D-mark against these other currencies, because such an appreciation would devalue the investment relative to the D-mark liabilities of the fund. Matching foreign currency holdings avoids exposure to this risk; non-matching requires a sufficient return on the overseas holding. It is, of course, possible for the fund to hedge its exposure by taking a forward position in foreign exchange, whether through the foreign exchange or, more likely, the swap market; but this transaction may add to investment costs.

EMU will alter the effect of this home bias in investment. This is because it enlarges appreciably the area in which funds can invest without exposure to foreign exchange risk. Thus, with EMU, German funds can invest in French securities without foreign exchange exposure. The range of securities in which the German fund can invest without exchange-rate risk is greatly increased; and similarly for investment funds in the other countries participating in EMU. Consequently the range of investment opportunities available to investment funds will increase, to the potential benefit of the beneficiaries of the funds. Security markets will become generally deeper and more liquid, and security markets in Europe will become more integrated.

Home bias because governments require it

This effect will be reinforced by a second. National regulations on investment funds in Europe constrain the choice over where to invest. German pension funds are required for reasons of prudential regulation to hold 75% of their investments in domestic-currency assets. After EMU, this regulation may well apply to euro, and not D-mark assets. Funds could then diversify out of German assets into the euro-denominated assets issued by other countries. Such national regulations may, in any case, have been removed as part of the single-market programme; but EMU should advance the process.

All is not clear, however. Much will depend on how national regulations are interpreted, which may require the intervention of the European Commission and the European Court. For example, national regulation may require that a certain percentage of the assets of a fund must be held in domestic assets. If so, EMU will relax this constraint only if other euro instruments are classified as domestic, not international. Since the justification for the restriction was usually currency risk, this is a reasonable interpretation. But governments and other domestic interests may resist this, preferring to interpret domestic as national. There is plenty of scope for dispute and delay in this area, but it is likely that the end result will be much more openness and freedom to invest across the euro area.

Hedging outside the euro zone

The impact of EMU on hedging and diversification of investment funds operating outside the euro zone, in the USA or Japan for example, is complex. Optimal investment strategies take advantage of the existence of a variety of currencies to diversify risk: with all one's investment eggs in the single-currency basket, the fund is exposed to major risk if something goes awry with that currency or its country or currency region. American funds place part of their portfolio in other currencies in order to guard against a major depreciation of the dollar and/or a collapse of asset values in the USA. Some of these funds are placed in assets denominated in the European currencies that will be transformed into the euro if EMU goes ahead.

The question is: will the introduction of the euro change the demand for these euro assets? Simple considerations of diversification would suggest a reduced demand: a single currency, rather than many, provides less risk diversification, and therefore makes euro assets less attractive overall than the assets they replaced. But this effect will probably be small or negligible. Some of the replaced currencies forming the euro have been fixed against the D-mark for some time and therefore have similar risk characteristics. The other currencies have been weaker, requiring a currency-risk premium: moving to a single currency may increase the attractiveness of the euro assets that replace these old weak-currency assets.

Ultimately, the attractiveness of euro assets for investors outside the euro zone will depend on macroeconomic performance under EMU. With strong growth in the EMU zone, euro equities will be attractive. With sound monetary policy from the ECB, euro-denominated fixed interest securities will be attractive. With a stagnant real economy and high inflation, euro assets may well be dumped.

The attractiveness of euro-denominated assets will determine not whether, in fact, they are held in portfolios, but rather the real returns and euro exchange rate required for them to be held. Thus if euro assets are unattractive internationally, the euro will fall against other currencies and euro interest rates will rise; if euro assets are attractive, the opposite will occur. Portfolio shifts in or out of the euro could have important implications, good or bad, for exchange-rate movements, international trade and the real economy, as discussed in Chapter 4.

Security markets

EMU will have important implications for the development of financial markets in Europe. It will create a large market in government debt all denominated in euros, and a large stock of euro equity. What will this market be like?

Bonds

Comparison is often drawn with the USA's market for federal debt, and the point is made that the euro market for government debt will be bigger. But this is not entirely the right comparison. America's market in treasury paper and federal debt is truly homogeneous: assets of the same terms and maturity are perfect substitutes, because they are all liabilities of the same agent, the US federal government. The market for euro debt will have similar instruments issued by different governments. Each government will have a different credit rating, and an important part of the business of the market will be the assessment of sovereign risk. (Only if the no-bail-out clause does not operate, or is expected not to operate, will this not be the case.)

In this respect, it will be like the market for debt issued by state governments in the USA. And in this market, it will be quite possible that a national government could face a higher risk premium than its national companies. (Hitherto, credit-rating agencies have adopted the rule that the credit rating of a company cannot be higher than that of its government, but under EMU that rule will be dropped.) Thus the high-debt governments of Belgium or Italy (if it participates) could have a lower credit rating than Belgian or Italian companies with strong balance sheets.

Some have argued that the EMU convergence frenzy in the second half of 1996, which saw the convergence of long-term interest rates among possible "ins" has gone too far. Thus it is suggested that financial markets have focused too much on the *convergence* of interest rates implied by the move to a single currency, and not enough on the *divergence* implied by different sovereign risk assessments. What is clear is that in the transition, which has already begun, getting these factors right will be critical to investment performance.

Equities Different considerations apply in the euro equity market. Such markets are accustomed to assessing company risk alongside currency risk for international investors. The euro will eliminate currency considerations, creating a deep market in euro equities. Over time, this is likely to develop further, as European countries are forced to move to funded pension arrangements and as corporate finance moves increasingly from traditional bank finance to securities.

Financial exchanges

Which financial centres will attract the business? With modern IT and communications capacity, there is no reason why securities trading should be in the country where it originates. Rather it will go through the financial centre or exchange that offers the most efficient trade, measured by the cost, speed and integrity of the transaction.

Hitherto within Europe, London has offered the most competitive trading environment, and has attracted much trade from other financial centres. Its competitive strength has rested on a number of factors: a large pool of financial expertise, a wide range of ancillary support services, light regulation of security trading, a favourable tax regime for expatriates moving to London, language (attractive to Americans, Japanese and others) and a location in a major political and cultural centre. On most—if not all—of these, Paris and Frankfurt have been uncompetitive. Virtuous circles are at work, reinforcing London's competitive strength: high volumes of trade allow London to offer competitive terms for trading; London's pre-eminence has made it easier to attract first-rate financial experts; the availability of expertise makes London attractive both for trading and locating an operation.

However, both Paris and Frankfurt are making strenuous efforts to catch up. They are modernising their trading systems, and France is relaxing its tax laws to persuade overseas experts to locate in Paris. The strategy is to use the changes and opportunities provided by EMU as the stimulus for change.

In this, they may be helped by two factors that act to London's disadvantage. First, there is the risk that London's preparations for EMU will be held back by uncertainty over the UK's participation and, despite the Bank of England's considerable efforts, by the difficulty the authorities have in giving a strong lead in these preparations while the question of UK participation or non-participation remains open. Second, there is the recent spate of financial scandals in London (though these have not been absent elsewhere). The danger is that these will weaken the reputation of the City, call into question the light regulatory framework, and lead to a loss of business to other financial centres. At the very least, the challenges by Paris and Frankfurt have been given a boost by the perception that London has vulnerabilities.

Nonetheless, while some business may be lost, London's strong competitive position is unlikely to be appreciably undermined, unless London plays its hand very badly: the reinforcing virtuous circles are likely to prove just too strong. Realisation of this could tempt the French and German governments to try to find protective barriers to ensure that some business remains at home. But such measures rarely work. Either they fail to bite because of the fluidity of financial market business, which allows it to get round or through most sorts of barrier. Or they do bite, but force the business offshore. The growth of the Eurodollar market reflected this: controls on the payment of interest in the USA meant that a large pool of international dollar liquidity developed in London to avoid the controls, thereby effectively undermining them.

It would be ironic, but not surprising, if discriminatory controls in the euro zone aimed at weakening London's position encouraged the development of a significant volume of euro trading outside the scope of the controls (the growth of a UK-Euro market along the lines of the early Euromarkets). Since French and German policy-makers acknowledge the force of this argument, discriminatory action of this kind will probably not occur.

Chapter 8 The future of Europe

We have seen in earlier chapters that one effect of EMU, if it happens and if it works, will be that participating economies will become more closely integrated. By removing the currency factor in intra-EMU trade and competition, one obstacle (of a non-tariff, non-regulatory kind) to head-on competition between European companies will be removed.

Drawing the political and economic strings together

But this is only part of the story. EMU is sometimes discussed as though the economic and political arguments are separate and additive, that one can simply add the economic arguments to the political ones to arrive at an overall view. In reality, economic and political forces interact; economic developments help to decide what becomes feasible politically. We saw in Chapter 2 that a single currency, unless abandoned, has usually generated a trend towards increased federal integration, though choices remain about the degree of federation. In the following chapters, we examined the economic implications of EMU in detail. In this concluding chapter, we draw together again the economic and political aspects.

At this broader level, a range of questions about EMU needs to be addressed. What does a partial EMU, involving some but not all EU members, imply for the future of the EU? Will it imply a progressive division into an inner core and an outer periphery, or will the "outs" in time join the "ins"? What might such divisions imply for the operations of the EU, and particularly the single market? What if EMU fails to function well, either continuing as a deflationary, high-unemployment bloc, or falling apart as countries withdraw? What would that imply for the future development of the EU? The EU is often compared with the wobbly cyclist, who falls off when momentum is lost. Will the EU return to the stagnation of the early 1980s before the single market project was launched, when many were questioning the dynamism and future of the EU? Or will the broad vision of European unity collapse altogether, with parts of the EU, in the form of subsets of countries, deciding to pursue deeper integration independently of other parts?

What these questions challenge is the commonly held assumption, particularly in the UK, that the single market is independent of EMU. The success or failure of EMU could have profound consequences for the single-market programme and for all countries in the EU, "ins" and "outs" alike.

It is also clear that these questions raise large imponderables, and therefore cannot be given a clear answer. The truth is that EMU may work well or badly, and may prove a great boost for the EU or its great undoing. These are issues on which reasonable people can and will disagree.

EMU and the nature of the EU

EMU will have enormous consequences for the future development of the EU. It is the first of the EU's great projects to envisage from the outset two tiers, them and us, and to embody this distinction in treaty form. The distinction is drawn in two ways: first, by allowing two countries (Denmark and the UK) an explicit and across-the-board opt-out from the main EMU arrangements; and second, by laying down explicit criteria for participation which could, in principle, indefinitely debar certain countries from participation. Previous initiatives, such as the common agricultural policy, the early tariff harmonisation process and the later single market, have allowed laggards in the process of implementation, as well as some individual tailoring of provisions, but have not allowed exemption altogether. The 1990 Schengen convention, which provided for early abolition of passport checks within a subset of EU countries (Benelux, France and Germany, since joined by all but the UK and Ireland), was a non-EU initiative, but was perhaps a harbinger of the deal over the Maastricht treaty that followed.

The turning-point at Maastricht?

The Maastricht treaty therefore signalled a great change in the direction of the EU. However, what exactly the signal means is open to debate. Some argue that it represents a shift away from a "table d'hôte" EU to an "à la carte" Union. For those of a less gastronomic bent, this is sometimes described as "variable geometry". Such arrangements allow each member to choose those elements of the EU that suit them best.

At the same time, a different trend is at work. The increase in qualified majority voting, as opposed to voting by unanimity, makes it harder for individual states to choose the parts of the EU they prefer. As a result of the EMU process, we see the growth of EMU-"ins" institutions: the ECB is the prime example, and another is the possibility of a subcommittee of Ecofin to oversee the operation of the stability and growth pact.

Other EMU-"ins" institutions may develop. This could lead to an inner and outer division within the EU, not just with respect to EMU but more widely. This would help to resolve the major problem of EU governance which will otherwise arise from enlargement of the EU both to the east and south. If this trend predominates, the EU may move towards an inner core of "ins" and an outer periphery of "outs". The "outs" would not have to assume all the requirements of membership, picking and choosing from the à la carte menu, but would have less decision-making power in consequence; while the "ins" would swallow the table d'hôte menu whole, and would have greater voting powers to influence EU directions.

Critics and opponents of this view of EU development point out that a move to a core/periphery structure in the EU would represent a fundamental change. It would therefore require a treaty amendment that any one member state could veto, thus making it unlikely. This is a strong point, and one that makes the development of the EU in this direction very difficult. The intergovernmental conference (IGC) set up to examine these very issues has made little progress, even under the highly effective Irish presidency up to December 1996. But this argument does not answer the fundamental question about the future governance of the Union. The institutional structures of the EU, set up for six member states, have now been stretched, with some modifications, to encompass 15. Can the same structures continue to work for a Union of 20 or 25 members?

If the present governance structures are not viable in the longer term, then pressures for change will inevitably rise. As the deficiencies of current decision-making become more apparent, it may not be easy for member states that oppose further integration and pooling of sovereignty to stand in the way of those who favour it. If they try to, the inner core could, in the extreme, go its own way by signing a new treaty. This is an unlikely event, but its possibility reduces the options of opponents to use the national veto to block constructive EU developments that command widespread support.

À la carte or table d'hôte?

It is unlikely that the future direction of the EU will be clear soon. These issues could take a decade or more to be worked out fully. What is really at stake is two separate visions of how cooperation between sovereign states should develop. On the one side, the à la carte approach suggests that bargains should be struck between member states on an issue-by-issue basis, with countries deciding whether or not to join in, based on whether the proposed bargain is judged to be in their interests. The table d'hôte approach, by contrast, requires commitment by countries to all agendas. Each country will participate if it derives benefit overall from the net impact of all the agreed policies, even though some individual policies may work against its interests.

At first sight, the à la carte approach might seem better. By choosing only the advantageous elements of the policies on offer, countries can get the best outcome. However, this need not be so. By linking together different agendas, the table d'hôte approach allows, at least in principle, for a wider range of bargains to be struck, with countries making concessions on one agenda to derive beneficial policies on another. In principle, the table d'hôte approach can generate much deeper cooperation.

That will not suit a number of countries, since it may lead eventually to a unitary European state. But it is not clear that these countries need or should stand in the way of those that wish to follow this route. It is right for the UK to argue for EU enlargement as a major policy priority, and to argue that deepening should not stand in its way. But it is also right for other countries to suggest that this requires a change in EU decision-making processes, to ensure that enlargement does not lead to organisational paralysis and does not stand in the way of further deepening.

The "outs" and the single market

If a partial EMU works successfully and a club of "ins" develops, how if at all might countries that remain outside be disadvantaged? In particular, how would such a development affect the single market provisions? There are four main possibilities.

- **Wholly benign.** EMU has no undesirable effects on single market developments, which proceed as rapidly and as far as if EMU had not occurred. There are therefore no undesirable effects on the "outs".

- **Somewhat benign.** The "ins" become the focus for integration, so that further development of the single market proceeds more rapidly among the "ins" than the "outs", with the "outs" missing out on these developments. However, the existing single market provisions are honoured.

- **Somewhat malign.** There is backsliding from the commitments of the single market by the "ins" against the "outs", through the less than rigorous enforcement of directives.

- **Wholly malign.** In this worst case, the "ins" insist on redrawing the single market provisions to reduce commitments to the "outs". This is a most unlikely outcome, since it would mean reneging on treaty commitments. But just as it is, in principle, feasible for reluctant members, such as the UK, to withdraw from its EU treaty commitments, so it is just conceivable that enthusiastic members might withdraw and regroup in order to move down the federal, integrative path more rapidly and without hindrance from the reluctant countries.

EMU and enlargement

Economic and strategic arguments

Perhaps the greatest challenge facing Europe at the end of the 20th century is to tie the central and east European countries of the former Soviet bloc into the EU. This need arises for both economic and strategic reasons. The removal of trade barriers would help the economic development of these countries, which since the Soviet collapse have gone through a traumatic economic restructuring. It would also benefit the economies of western Europe, as the removal of tariff barriers and quotas would yield the benefits of freer trade.

But the more important objective of such integration would be political: by lending support to these countries through economic integration and demonstrating the willingness of the market economies of western Europe to help them, the EU would help to stabilise these countries politically and socially. This part of the world has been extremely turbulent over the past century and more, particularly when an empire collapsed—the Ottoman Empire, the Austro-Hungarian Empire and most recently the Soviet Union. Such explosions have had a huge impact on the rest of Europe. The price for neglecting this issue could well be high.

Enlargement to the east raises difficult questions. These are poor economies with large agricultural sectors and low industrial productivity. Full integration with the EU countries would impose an impossible burden of adjustment on these economies. Flexible integration is needed to allow these countries to integrate gradually as their economic performance improves. But how far should such integration go? Will it include only the central and east European countries, or will it stretch as far as the Ukraine or even Russia itself?

The IGC, which is addressing issues of EU governance, is more or less stalled and unlikely to shed much light on these questions. The main focus of EU members and of the European Commission is inward, on the question of preparing for EMU. This could easily absorb their energies up to 2002 and beyond, nearly a decade and a half after the dismantling of the Berlin Wall. If so, the prospects for enlargement are dismal. And if the EMU process runs into trouble for any reason, EU energies will be devoted to fixing it, again pushing enlargement off the agenda. Critics of EMU therefore have a strong point when they argue that EMU is a major diversion from the key policy issue facing the EU.

Proponents of EMU may reply that monetary union is essential to the future dynamism of the EU (an issue examined in earlier chapters), and that only a dynamic EU can respond adequately to the challenge of enlargement. Moreover, if EMU does result in a shift in EU governance structures towards a core/associate structure, then this will make it easier to integrate new members as associates committed to flexible integration. The problem with this is one of timescale. How long will all this take?

The structure of Europe's economy

Tax, labour and regulatory challenges

Enlargement is one key undertaking that is being, and may continue to be, neglected because of EMU. But it is not the only one. Many see the EU economy as suffering from serious structural problems that need to addressed. These include burdensome taxes, especially in the form of the high overhead costs of hiring labour; inappropriate regulation of labour markets; excessive regulation in many product markets; continued state involvement in many sectors; and state subsidies that encourage inefficiencies. There is also the concern that state commitments in the form of unfunded pension rights will require further tax rises in the future, adding to these problems (though the UK record points to other possibilities).

These effects will all be reinforced if the introduction of the euro increases the role of cross-country wage comparisons in European wage-setting. If wages in all parts of the EMU zone move increasingly in lock-step, because of the ease of comparison between countries, then EMU implies more wage rigidity and less labour-market flexibility.

All such rigidities will impede the medium- and longer-term growth of the European economies and impair Europe's capacity to compete internationally. A concern about EMU is that it will exacerbate these problems by:

- leading to greater bureaucracy and rigidities. EMU may spread the regulation/subsidy/dependency culture through harmonisation;
- diverting attention from competitiveness, market flexibility, deregulation;
- generating an inward focus, leading to a failure to keep up with international competition.

The danger is that EMU will reinforce the EU in its move down the road to excessive harmonisation and regulation. EMU, if it happens, will remove the possibility of adjustment through exchange-rate changes, and will therefore throw greater weight on to labour-market adjustment. In short, it is argued,

EMU will reinforce excessive regulation and labour market rigidities, whereas its success requires the very opposite.

A cure for Eurosclerosis?

Optimists reply that exchange-rate flexibility offers no way out of these problems. Devaluation to deal with problems of excessive product and labour market rigidities generates inflation in the longer term, not lower unemployment, since unemployment in the long run is determined by structural factors. Also, EMU is forcing a reconsideration of the high-tax, high-borrowing, high-regulatory tendencies of European countries. The need to meet the Maastricht criteria is leading to adjustments, some cosmetic to be sure but others more far-reaching. There is a growing appreciation among policy-makers that countries may avoid problems of structural unemployment within the EMU zone by addressing the problem of structural rigidities in the European economies.

This could be interpreted as a do-or-die approach: lock countries into EMU where they have no choice but to reform if they wish to prosper. This is a risky strategy, but one not without merit: European policy-makers have the opportunity to present major policy changes to their electorates as necessary to make EMU work. There is the real possibility that European countries will move more towards liberalisation as a result of EMU than they would have done otherwise. And advocates of EMU can also argue with force that the likely backlash resulting from the failure of the EMU project would represent a major setback to the process of liberalisation and deregulation.

Four plausible scenarios

Earlier in this report, we examined the many factors that will determine the future of EMU and with it the future development of the European economy and the EU. As the analysis has made clear, these factors are complex and uncertain. No one can know with certainty the impact of EMU, whether for good or bad; those who claim otherwise mislead. The debate over EMU is one about the balance of probabilities, on which reasonable people can disagree. The one certainty is that EMU is a risky venture. Some might argue against it on the grounds that it is wrong to take risks with the future of the EU. But all major political ventures involve risk, and the question is just how much, to be balanced against the potential gains—again an issue on which reasonable people can differ.

The analysis in previous chapters has taken positions on parts of the debate over EMU, where we consider some arguments to be false or over simple. So far we have not taken a position on the overall development of EMU, but instead have discussed the issues at stake as objectively and dispassionately as possible. The aim has been to enable readers to understand the complex issues at stake, and to make up their own minds. It would vitiate that aim, and undermine the objective nature of this report, were we to come down for or against EMU, or to argue that it will "succeed" or "fail". These terms themselves mean different things to different people. Economic factors need to be weighed against political ones, long-term developments against short-term, and so on. The weights assigned to these different factors are also matters on which reasonable people can differ.

In emphasising the uncertainties over EMU, we are certainly not arguing that it is impossible to take a view on the issue. Responsible citizens need to do just that. But coming to a view requires probabilities and value-judgements to be weighed alongside facts: the objectivity we aspire to in the report can take you only so far towards a conclusion. Since EMU is an uncertain venture, we think it helpful to consider alternative scenarios. Below, we develop four, based on two different dimensions:

- whether EMU happens or not;
- whether the EU prospers or stagnates.

In our view, each of these scenarios represents a possible development for the EU over the next decade or more, and is therefore worthy of serious consideration. Each scenario is, of course, a stylised simplification, and actual developments in the EU could combine some elements of different scenarios. But it is helpful to consider the different scenarios as polar cases along a two-dimensional spectrum of possibilities.

Four scenarios for EMU

	Europe stagnates	**Europe prospers**
EMU abandoned	*Scenario l:* Europe stalled, EU divided	*Scenario 2:* Single market triumphant, EU unified
EMU happens	*Scenario 3:* The core humbled, EU divided	*Scenario 4:* EMU triumphant, EU unified

No EMU: Europe stalled and the EU divided

Scenario 1

This is the scenario that vindicates the bicycle theory of the EU. Growth in Europe remains low over the next two years, reflecting a tight monetary stance from the Bundesbank and budget cuts as countries try to meet the Maastricht criteria. The result is that, despite budget cuts, only two or three countries satisfy the Maastricht criteria. Attempts to fudge the numbers by accounting tricks and a flexible interpretation are foiled as German opinion shifts against EMU, and Bonn is forced to insist on a strict interpretation to avoid appeal to the German constitutional court. This means that EMU can proceed only with a small minority of countries. Faced with this prospect, the excluded majority vote for a delayed start. The resulting acrimonious dispute sets member states against each other, and in effect buries the project.

The failure to proceed with EMU adds to recessionary tendencies. The high debt/high inflation countries, which were enjoying the pre-EMU virtuous circle as interest rates fell to German levels, experience a sharp reversal as their exchange rates fall, long-term interest rates spring back up and governments are forced to raise short-term interest rates to prevent a resurgence of inflation.

Scenario 1

No EMU: Europe stalled, EU divided

- Most countries fail to meet the Maastricht criteria.
- Increasing popular discontent with the prospect of the euro, especially in Germany.
- EMU is initially postponed and then indefinitely postponed.
- The high-debt countries experience sharp rise in short and long-term interest rates, worsening fiscal problems.
- Considerable acrimony among EU members.
- Lack of progress in further implementation of single-market provisions and in liberalisation of EU telecoms and energy markets.
- Failure to tackle problems of structural rigidities in Europe.
- EU countries stagnate amid mountains of debt.
- EU loses its direction and momentum.
- EU failure to address the issue of enlargement to the east.

These countries are forced back into the vicious circle of high interest rates, worsening fiscal deficits and debt. Their economies, already weak, slide into recession as high interest rates stall investment and consumer confidence. Unemployment rises, worsening the problems of public finances as tax revenues stagnate and unemployment benefit payments rise. In the longer term, failure to address the issue of unfunded pension commitments leads to a further twist of the debt spiral as the payouts from pay-as-you-go state pension arrangements rise. Diverging inflation trends lead to volatile intra-European exchange rates, both real and nominal. This exacerbates trade frictions within the single market.

The failure to agree on EMU casts a long shadow over other policy initiatives. High and rising unemployment leads to a reluctance to open up markets, particularly the hitherto protected national markets of telecoms, energy and air transport. Existing single market provisions are observed only half-heartedly, and there is unwillingness to consider new developments. Attempts by the European Commission and Court to enforce compliance meet with widespread opposition in many countries.

In addition the EU fails to address two other key issues. Reform of welfare systems to increase labour market flexibility loses momentum as each country blames other member states for blocking EMU and causing economic stagnation. Enlargement to the east is also blocked, and the EU maintains high protective barriers against this part of Europe, to the detriment of itself and eastern Europe.

In the next decade the EU's standing in the world erodes further. This leads to a questioning of the value of the EU, rather as in the early 1980s. But this time the questioning is more serious: many member states start to look at other parts of the world, particularly the dynamic parts of Asia, to develop trade links. However, this is largely unsuccessful: dynamic economies elsewhere look for links with other dynamic economies, not the debt-ridden, sclerotic economies of western Europe. The Old World is irremediably senile.

No EMU: the single market triumphant and the EU unified

Scenario 2

In this scenario also, growing opposition to EMU leads the EU to defer the project. But this is done proactively, in a spirit of cooperation and agreement. It is generally agreed that it is better to focus on the three issues of liberalisation of the European economy, EU governance and enlargement, before introducing a single currency. Although there are doubters about this change of direction for the EU, the political opposition to EMU in many countries leads each government to agree that it makes sense. EU countries therefore set about tackling the other agendas with purpose and harmony.

Scenario 2

No EMU: single market triumphant, EU unified

- Increasing lack of support for EMU leads EU countries to defer EMU and concentrate on other policy initiatives.
- The move to fiscal responsibility continues, reducing problems of excessive deficits and debt.
- All countries succeed in achieving low inflation, despite the abandonment of the euro.
- Major moves to liberalise European telecoms, energy and airline markets and to pursue energetically the implementation of all single market directives.
- Reform of European benefit systems and undue labour market regulation leads to greater flexibility of labour markets.
- Result is a dynamic growing European economy, with falling unemployment.
- A more confident EU addresses the issue of enlargement to the east.

Thus the move to fiscal responsibility continues, reducing problems of excessive deficits and debt, and member states act to scale down future unfunded pension liabilities to manageable proportions. The dangers of high and rising debt levels, apparent in Scenario 1, are avoided. Falling deficits and debt levels maintain confidence that all countries will enjoy low inflation, despite deferment of the discipline of the ECB, and thereby help to keep down interest rates even in those countries with high debt. This maintains the virtuous circle of convergence and avoids the vicious circle of Scenario 1. Converging inflation trends avoid currency instability and therefore the divisive effects on the single market that show up in Scenario 1. Low inflation and interest rates sustain growth, thereby maintaining the buoyancy of government finances and smoothing the adjustment to low fiscal deficits and a prudent fiscal stance.

The resulting prosperity, coupled with the spirit of harmony, provides the basis for major moves to liberalise European telecoms, energy and airline markets and to pursue energetically the implementation of all single market directives. It also facilitates the progressive reform of European benefit systems and labour market regulation, leading to greater flexibility of labour markets.

Thus in this scenario the virtuous circle of liberalisation and prosperity works to the benefit of all countries. The result is a dynamic, growing European economy with falling unemployment, strengthening still further Europe's sound fiscal position. Against this background, a confident EU is able to address the issue of enlargement to the east, allowing this part of Europe to share in the prosperity of western Europe, anchoring eastern Europe to the western market economies and avoiding political and social unrest. A strong, unified Europe can compete effectively against all comers.

EMU: the core humbled and the EU divided

Scenario 3

In this scenario, a political compromise leads to a group of 6-10 countries proceeding to EMU on time on January 1, 1999. In spite of fudging of the Maastricht criteria, Chancellor Kohl is able to sell the deal to the German people, on the basis that otherwise EMU will not happen and Europe will be divided (the arguments of Scenario 1). Motivated by continued EMU euphoria and concerned not to be left behind, several other countries join two or three years later, before the problems of EMU have become fully apparent.

Scenario 3

EMU: the core humbled, EU divided

- 6-10 countries join EMU.
- EMU works badly.
- Instabilities in transition: ECB hits technical problems in running euro monetary policy.
- Conflicts between ECB and Ecofin lead to instability of the euro against other currencies, and dollar:yen volatility.
- Unemployment high and rising in some areas, because of structural rigidities strengthened by EMU.
- Debt levels climb; debt traps re-emerge.
- General European stagnation.
- Excessive bureaucracy: failure to tackle rigidities.
- Enlargement issue avoided, so that Europe as a whole is divided.
- The "outs" fare better than the "ins" but still suffer from the stagnation of the EMU core.
- Political pressures build for the abandonment of EMU and the restoration of national currencies.
- Growing disenchantment with EU integration undermines commitment to the single market.

For a variety of reasons EMU works badly, though it takes some years for this to be evident. The initial fudging of the convergence criteria for participation means that debt and deficit levels remain high in a number of participating countries. The ECB hits technical problems in running euro monetary policy, failing to judge correctly the shifts in money holdings induced by the introduction of the euro, so that the operation of euro monetary policy is excessively volatile. This is exacerbated by conflicts between the ECB and Ecofin over the operation of fiscal Policy. The imposition of fines on persistent high-deficit countries, under the stability and growth pact (ill-named under this scenario) generates major political rows. This leads to instability of the euro against other currencies, and associated instability in the dollar:yen rate, as foreign exchange markets speculate on alternative resolutions of these conflicts.

Along with these technical difficulties, unemployment in the EMU zone remains high and on an upward trend in some areas, because of structural rigidities in the European economy and exchange-rate inflexibility caused by EMU. High and rising payments of unemployment benefits, added to rising unfunded pension commitments for an ageing population, put growing strain on government finances. As a result, debt levels climb and the debt traps reemerge in many participating countries. The result is general stagnation within the EMU area.

Alongside these macroeconomic trends, the introduction of the euro leads to more, not less, regulation and excessive bureaucracy. The EMU members fail to tackle the excessive rigidities in their economies. The enlargement issue is ducked, so that Europe as a whole remains divided and political opinion in eastern Europe moves against the EU as it continues to exclude these economies from trade. Growing disenchantment with EU integration undermines commitment to the single market, and there is considerable backsliding from existing commitments and an unwillingness to consider new liberalisation measures (as in Scenario 1).

Against this background, the few countries that stood aside from EMU fare better than the "ins", but are not immune to the stagnation of the EMU area. There develops over time considerable political disaffection with EMU, and political pressure builds for its abandonment and the restoration of national currencies. In some countries this takes a strongly nationalistic flavour, with calls for independence and self-determination and some countries leaving the EU. As in a Greek tragedy, EMU achieves the opposite of what its advocates want: the division and break-up of the EU and the resurgence of nationalism.

EMU triumphant and the EU unified

Scenario 4

As in Scenario 3, between six and ten countries proceed to EMU in 1999, and others follow, so that most EU countries have adopted the euro by 2002. Although the process involves some fudging of the Maastricht criteria, this does not present a problem: countries continue to make major fiscal adjustments afterwards, helped by low interest rates and the resulting growth in the European economy. Despite teething problems, the transition to the euro works smoothly and the ECB quickly establishes a reputation for the sound conduct of euro monetary policy, balancing the need to maintain low and stable inflation against the need to look after the real economy. Low interest rates help the European economy to revive and unemployment fall. With a strong economy, fiscal imbalances quickly disappear: concerns that EMU will prove debt-ridden prove unfounded. The stability and growth pact lives up to its name, and, like all the best threats, the provision to levy fines on recalcitrant high borrowing countries remains unexercised in the background.

Scenario 4

EMU triumphant, EU unified

- 6-10 countries proceed to EMU in 1999, and others follow: most EU countries adopt euro by 2002.
- Transition to euro works smoothly.
- No major macroeconomic problems: the European economy revives and unemployment falls.
- ECB establishes an early and strong reputation.
- No institutional conflicts between ECB and Ecofin.
- Euro widely adopted as vehicle currency.
- European competitiveness tackled by flexibility and deregulation.
- No creeping protectionism.
- Debt and deficit problems solved.
- Some limited accretion of powers to Brussels, but no general federalism: an open decentralised Europe (on the Swiss model).
- A strong EU addresses the issue of enlargement, avoiding conflicts to the east.

Nor do fears of institutional conflicts between the ECB and Ecofin materialise: the effective pragmatism of the ECB together with continued growth and falling unemployment means that concerns by national finance ministers, and by electorates more generally, about the ECB's autonomy and independence remain muted. The lack of instabilities in euro monetary policy mean that the euro is widely adopted as a vehicle currency. Potential instabilities resulting from this between the euro and the dollar, and hence the yen and the dollar, are avoided through appropriate management by the G7.

Against this benign macroeconomic environment, the EU has the confidence and ability to tackle its other major policy agendas. Thus the issue of European competitiveness is addressed by policies to promote flexibility and appropriate deregulation. The single market framework is respected and enhanced: there is no problem of creeping protectionism. There is growing federalism, but not of a sweeping kind: with agreed changes in EU governance, some extra powers accrue to Brussels, but these are limited and subsidiarity is generally observed. The EU avoids the dangers of excessive federalism, but aims towards an open, decentralised Europe on the Swiss model. Importantly, a confident EU pushes ahead with enlargement, thereby avoiding conflicts to the east. The single currency provides the underpinning for a strong, stable and united Europe, proving the critics of EMU wrong.

A tentative conclusion

What the author thinks

The reader who has reached this far will know quite a lot about the author's view of EMU: that it is a risky but momentous venture that will determine the future development of Europe over the coming decades, for better or worse; and that the uncertainties about the EMU process are such that no single forecast is worth a great deal since it is too unreliable. The scenarios just elaborated are intended to illustrate that uncertainty.

Despite this, the reader is entitled to ask what the author would say if pressed to make a best-guess forecast about EMU. The author's views are on the public record, so it would be disingenuous to avoid answering. In summary, the author's position on EMU is best described as that of the "sceptical pro", a suitably ambiguous phrase.

In the absence of a single currency, there is a risk that exchange-rate variability *will* limit the development of the single market, and that the EU will stagnate. To that extent, we side with those who see the single currency as important for the realisation of the single market. Thus if EMU does not proceed, while we hope that Scenario 2 can be realised, we fear that Scenario 1 is somewhat more probable.

EMU will go ahead—

We think that it is more likely that EMU will proceed, with up to ten countries participating in the first wave and with a few others following later. In this event, we think it likely that the technical problems of the transition will be resolved, and that the ECB will quite quickly develop a reputation for the sound conduct of monetary policy, so that the euro will become a firm, if not a hard, currency and the EMU zone will enjoy low inflation. But we also think it likely that the problem of high European unemployment will remain, and possibly intensify in some parts of the EMU zone. This is because of the constraints placed on the flexibility of national fiscal policy as a consequence of the inaptly named stability and growth pact. Thus our views of the most likely (but, to repeat, very uncertain) outcome combines elements of both Scenario 3 and 4.

In time, though not quickly, continued high unemployment could undermine the authority of the ECB and lead to pressures for change. The future of EMU and of the EU will depend on how European leaders respond to this challenge. A failure to respond could easily send the EU down the path to Scenario 3, with nationalist forces leading to a slow unravelling of EMU and the EU itself. The wrong response, such as trying to force the ECB to adopt a looser monetary policy, with the consequence of higher inflation, could be equally destructive for the future of the EU. Yet the unaccountable nature of the ECB leaves it a target for such pressures.

What will be required is appropriate reform of fiscal, welfare and labour market arrangements within the EU to remove undue rigidities in European economies. This would in part require the reform of the stability and growth pact, allowing individual nations greater flexibility of fiscal deficits over the cycle, permitting automatic fiscal stabilisers to work whilst simultaneously guarding against recourse to excessive government debt in the longer term. It would also involve the reform, and possible expansion, of current fiscal transfers between EU members, so as to target them more directly to tackle the problem of the differential cyclical element in unemployment across the EU. This implies further cuts in Common Agricultural Policy spending, which accounts for the bulk of such transfers at present. It may well mean an evolution over time towards a form of fiscal federalism, as has happened in other evolving monetary unions. It would also imply reform of those aspects of national labour market and welfare policy that discourage employment opportunities in order to tackle the structural aspects of European unemployment.

Such reforms, if successfully implemented, would lead the EU towards Scenario 4. Those concerned with national sovereignty will note that the growth of fiscal transfers is yet another step down the road to federalism. That is true, but members of the EU have considerable choice as to how far that goes. A single currency with growing fiscal transfers between nations certainly represents a move towards federalism. But Europe (and the UK with it) has already moved a long way down that road, and the further movement need not be large, especially if the principle of subsidiarity is applied strictly to prospective, but more importantly existing, European policy programmes.

—with appropriate policies Europe could be an economic dynamo—

With the right set of policy responses, the EU could therefore travel in the direction of Scenario 4, towards a sustainable and well-functioning monetary union. With appropriate policies, Europe could become an economic dynamo. Without them, it will continue to decline and lose out to other parts of the world, notably Asia. Moreover, the EU must also face the need to open to the eastern part of Europe, to avoid the political and social unrest that will otherwise result. Getting these policies right will not be easy, and predicting that this will happen would be rash. If EMU proceeds, the lack of exchange-rate flexibility will mean that regional unemployment and industrial balance will emerge as even more important policy issues than hitherto. The future of the EU will depend on its capacity to address these fundamental issues. Much will depend on whether there are European leaders in the next decade with the right strategic vision for Europe and the capacity to realise it. But that requires a vigorous and informed public debate throughout the members of the EU, so that these crucial issues are at the forefront of European politics.

—but the risks are great

Europe faces momentous developments over the next few years and in the first decade of the next century. EMU is a risky venture: ensuring that it works well will be fundamental to the future prosperity of the region and the well-being of its people.

Glossary

Central bank Banks' and government's bank; eg Bundesbank, Bank of England; influences interest rates and/or money supply by buying and selling government bonds; central banks participating in EMU must be independent.

Convergence criteria Fiscal and monetary benchmarks to be met before a country may join EMU.

Council of Ministers EU forum for ministerial meetings with legislative powers.

EC European Community; comprises three component communities: ECSC, EEC and Euratom.

ECB European Central Bank; will set and implement monetary policy for EMU, including influencing euro's exchange rates; headquartered in Frankfurt, it will use central banks as agents.

ECJ European Court of Justice; EU court of appeal and interpreter of the treaties; sits in Luxembourg.

ECSC European Coal and Steel Community; one of three original components of EC.

Ecu European currency unit; EU accounting unit calculated by weighting and averaging the currencies of 12 of the EU's member countries; when the euro is launched, it will be worth Ecu1. In mid-January 1997 Ecu1 was worth $1.23, DM1.94 and £0.73.

EEA European Economic Area; single market comprising EU, Norway, Iceland and Liechtenstein.

EEC European Economic Community; free-trade area of the EU, with common external import duties.

EMI European Monetary Institute; precursor of ECB.

EMS European Monetary System; set up in 1979 to coordinate monetary and exchange rate policies, latter through a device called exchange rate mechanism (ERM).

EMU Economic and monetary union; participants adopt single currency and pool the running of their monetary policies. Maastricht treaty provides for EMU of qualifying EU member countries, with Denmark and UK being allowed to opt out if they wish.

EP European Parliament; meets mainly in Strasbourg.

ERM Exchange rate mechanism; most crucial and visible facet of EMS, linking participants' currencies within defined bands.

EU European Union of 15 countries; comprises EC and two other "pillars", a common foreign and security policy (CFSP) and cooperation in justice and interior affairs.

Euratom European Atomic Energy Community, one of three original components of the EC.

euro EMU's planned single currency; will be worth Ecu1.

European Commission Initiator of EU policy and administrative organ, based in Brussels.

European Council Summit of leaders of EU member states.

Fiscal deficit Gap between government's spending and revenue; financed by borrowing.

GDP Gross domestic product; sum of all output produced by economic activity within a country.

IGC Intergovernmental conference; sitting since 1996 to review workings of Maastricht treaty, with constitutional reform topping agenda.

Labour market rigidities Various factors preventing wages from responding sharply to changes in supply of and demand for labour, and inhibiting people from moving to where their skills are most in demand.

Legal tender Money that is legally valid for payment of debts; must be accepted for that purpose when offered.

Maastricht treaty International agreement signed in Maastricht, the Netherlands in 1992; lays down plans for EMU.

Money supply National sum of coins, notes, bank deposits and other "money" available to buy goods and services; various definitions exist; along with other factors, influences inflation.

QMV Qualified majority voting; 62 out of 87 weighted votes in Council of Ministers, sufficient to adopt most EU legislation. Other legislation requires unanimity.

Real terms Figures adjusted to exclude the effect of inflation.

Single market Central objective of EU since 1986, defined as "an area without internal frontiers in which the free movement of goods, persons, services and capital is ensured"; also known as internal market .

Stability and growth pact International agreement under which countries participating in EMU will be obliged to limit size of their fiscal deficits, under pain of heavy financial penalties.

Subsidiarity Principle introduced by Maastricht treaty that EU should take action only where the proposed objectives cannot be sufficiently achieved by member states on their own.

TARGET Trans-European Automated Real-time Gross settlement Express Transfer system linking national bank clearing systems.

Sources: *The EIU European yearbook 1994-95; International Dictionary of Finance,* The Economist Books; Webster's *New Collegiate Dictionary*, Merriman Webster.

Appendix 1 How the EU's powers have developed

*by Alan Riley**

1951: the European Coal and Steel Community (ECSC)

The overriding aim of the architects of the first European treaty, Jean Monnet and Robert Schuman, six years after the end of the Second World War, was clear. In the preamble to the Treaty of Paris, the six signatories (France, Germany, Italy and Benelux) resolved "to end the bloody conflicts that divided us". Their means of reconciling German prosperity to French security was to take the two most important materials for waging mid-20th century wars, coal and steel, and place them under a common supranational authority.

The ECSC treaty created a supranational executive, the High Authority, an Advisory Council of the ministers of the member states, an Assembly of European Parliamentarians and a Court of Justice. Although the outlines of the institutional structure were retained in all future European treaties, the relative power positions changed. The Council, even before the advent of the EEC treaty, took on an increasingly dominant role in the decision-making processes of the Community. The High Authority and its successor, the European Commission, increasingly played second fiddle to the Council; it is still confusing to outside observers on many occasions as to whether the Commission is acting as mere secretariat to the Council, as European honest broker-cum-policy fixer, or as a true European executive. The Court of Justice, by contrast, continues to play a vital role in setting out the rules of the Community's binding legal order and ensuring the application of legislation adopted by the Council. Increasingly, the European Parliament (which informally changed its name from an Assembly in 1962 and formally from 1987) through successive treaty amendments has taken on a greater share of legislative power from the Council.

The Paris treaty came into force in August 1952, for a period of 50 years. The High Authority was granted powers to create a common market in coal and steel. In addition, it was granted powers to supervise prices, wages, investment and competition in the coal and steel sectors.

The High Authority had limited success in creating a common market and ensuring effective competition. However, it did resolve the conflicts over coal

* Alan Riley is a regular contributor to the EIU's newsletter *Business Europe*.

and steel between France and Germany and in so doing removed the main obstacle to economic partnership between the nations of continental western Europe.

The ECSC treaty will expire in August 2002. The provisions of the EEC treaty and its successor treaties will then apply to coal and steel.

1957: the European Economic Community (EEC)

In order to further European reconciliation and reap tangible economic benefits from economic integration, the member states of the ECSC were prepared to consider proposals for a much wider economic agreement. This consensus led to the calling of the Messina conference in 1955 and the drafting of the all-encompassing European Economic Community treaty (Treaty of Rome) and the sectoral European Atomic Energy Community (Euratom) treaty.

The purpose of the EEC treaty was to establish a common market among the member states covering all forms of economic activity. Powers were transferred to the EEC from the member states to create freedom of movement of goods, services, capital, labour and businesses. The EEC was also given the power to create common policies in such fields as competition, transport and social policy. In addition, the treaty provided for the creation of a customs union, a common external tariff and a common external trade policy. The Euratom community was given the power to create the conditions necessary for the speedy establishment and growth of the nuclear industries.

Both the EEC and Euratom treaties were concluded for an unlimited period. Withdrawal is impossible save by agreement of the member states and subsequent amendment of the respective treaties. Hence, in 1982 when Greenland withdrew from all three Communities, its withdrawal was executed by agreement of the member states and subsequent amendment of all three treaties.

Originally, although a single Court of Justice was established for all three Communities, each community otherwise had its own separate European institutions. By the 1965 merger treaty a single Council, Commission and Parliament were established for all three Communities. Despite the institutional merger the three Communities remain legally distinct.

1966: the Luxembourg compromise and Eurosclerosis

The first few years of the new EEC were very successful. The early 1960s saw enormous growth in intra-Community trade, and the abolition of internal customs duties and creation of the common outer tariff were completed ahead of the 1968 deadline.

However, these successes were overshadowed in 1965 by France's adoption of the "empty chair" policy of then president Charles de Gaulle and the subsequent 1966 Luxembourg compromise. The compromise was essentially an agreement to disagree between General de Gaulle, an ardent believer in the independence and integrity of the nation state, and more integrationist

Europeans over majority voting. The compromise itself reiterated the belief of the Five in the value of majority voting. However, the statement in the compromise that "when very important issues are at stake, discussions must be continued until unanimous agreement is reached", did serious damage to the ability of the member states to act together. Following the enlargement of the Communities in 1973, the Luxembourg compromise was seized upon by all member states to protect their national positions.

Not all progress was undermined by the compromise. The Communities were enlarged to include the UK, Ireland and Denmark in 1973. The member states agreed in 1970 on an effective budget reform. The Parliament was given greater powers over the budget. The financing of the budget itself was transformed. Instead of the member states providing direct financial contributions, the Communities established a system of own resources. In future, they would be largely financed from customs duties, agricultural levies and a percentage of value-added tax. The early 1970s also saw the beginnings of common policies in fields such as regional development, social affairs and the environment.

In 1978 as a result of the initiative of the Commission president, Roy Jenkins, the European monetary system (EMS) was launched. This included a mechanism for stabilising exchange rates (the exchange-rate mechanism, ERM) which proved successful in the mid- to late-1980s in stabilising European currencies, until the debacle of September 1992.

The late 1970s also saw an agreement by the member states to hold the first direct elections to the European Parliament. These took place in June 1979 and foreshadowed the increasing importance of the Parliament in the decision-making processes of the Communities. In 1981, Greece became the tenth member state.

Despite these successes, it cannot be denied that the Luxembourg compromise significantly set back the Communities. By the early 1970s almost 1,000 legislative proposals were blocked by the veto. Morale in the Commission had plummeted. The negative effects of the compromise were compounded by the oil crisis and the consequent recessions of the 1970s. Recession and increasing unemployment made it far more difficult for member states to agree upon effective common policies. The paralysis of the Communities' institutions led commentators to coin the term "Eurosclerosis" to describe the impotence of the EEC.

1986: the relaunch of Europe and the Single European Act (SEA)

In addition to the problems created by the Luxembourg compromise and the recessions of the 1970s, a significant barrier to progress was the debate over the British budget contribution. As a result of the UK's later accession, the system of financing the Communities did not take account of the impact it would have on the UK. In effect, the UK made substantial over-payments to the Communities. The issue of the British budget question (BBQ—known familiarly in Brussels as "the bloody British question") monopolised the attention of the Community leadership in the late 1970s and early 1980s. However, following a successful European summit at Fontainebleau in 1984, this issue was resolved.

With the resolution of the BBQ, with the European economies moving out of recession and calls from business leaders to complete the common market, the time was ripe for new proposals for common European action. The new Commission president, Jacques Delors, with the new internal market commissioner, Lord Cockfield, proposed to complete the common market. In a famous White Paper Lord Cockfield identified 268 measures which if adopted by the end of 1992 would lead to the creation of a genuine single market. The White Paper was discussed and approved at the Milan summit in June 1985.

Clearly, if 268 measures were to be adopted by 1992, the member states would have to agree to amend the EEC treaty, introduce more majority voting and agree to at least limit the application of the Luxembourg compromise. This led to the calling of a treaty-amending conference (in EC jargon known as an "intergovernmental conference" or IGC). The conference met in Brussels and Luxembourg in September 1985 and drafted what came to be known as the Single European Act (SEA).

The SEA was approved by the leaders of the member states in February 1986 and came into force, following national ratification, in July 1987. It resulted in four important developments.

Introduction of more qualified majority voting. The SEA provided far more opportunity for qualified majority voting (QMV) on legislative matters, particularly in relation to single market issues but also for some social issues, such as health and safety.

Acceptance of variable geometry A *quid pro quo* for QMV was the acceptance of variable geometry. Prior to the introduction of the SEA, the law of the Communities had to be applied uniformly in all member states. The SEA recognised scope for variable geometry in the EEC treaty. New legislation could now be applied differently and at different times in different member states.

Institutionalisation of the European Council. Although the heads of government and heads of state of the member states had been meeting regularly since the Paris summit in 1974, there was no official recognition in the EEC treaty of their role. This was despite the fact that it was often the decisions of this group which led to effective action by the Communities. The SEA recognised the existence of this group as the European Council but accorded it no direct powers.

Recognition of European political cooperation. Equally, the SEA gave institutional form to European political cooperation (EPC), which, with some notable failures such as reaction to the 1973 oil crisis, had been developing between the member states since the late 1960s. In order to ensure that member state control was maintained over sensitive external political matters, EPC was placed outside the institutional machinery of the Communities.

The single-market programme set out in Cockfield's White Paper, and provided by the SEA with the means to act, was remarkably successful. By the end of 1992 more than 250 of the 268 measures to create a genuine single market had been adopted. Even more remarkably, the single-market programme had engendered a degree of enthusiasm among business and citizens for European integration unseen even in the earliest days of the EEC.

The success of the Communities led to more interest and investment from outside Europe and more interest in membership and participation from within. The membership of the Communities increased to 12 states with the accession of Spain and Portugal in January 1986. The European Free Trade Area (EFTA) states began negotiations for a multilateral agreement which would permit them to benefit from the single market. Subsequently a European Economic Area (EEA) agreement came into force in January 1994, embracing the EEC and ECSC with Austria, Finland, Iceland, Liechtenstein, Norway and Sweden.

The SEA exists as a separate treaty from the EEC, ECSC and Euratom treaties. The treaty stands on it own save where it expressly amends the existing EEC treaty. It was concluded for an unlimited period.

1991: Maastricht and the Treaty on European Union (TEU)

At the height of the Commission's 1980s reputation, the president, Jacques Delors, began planning the next stage of European economic integration. At the 1988 Hanover summit the leaders of the member states agreed to convene a committee chaired by Mr Delors to examine the possibility of European monetary union. The Delors committee reported in 1989 and recommended a three-stage plan for the creation of economic and monetary union (EMU).

As some member states would not support EMU without further institutional reforms, and EMU itself required treaty amendments, two parallel treaty revision conferences were convened in December 1990. The member states finally signed a single Treaty on European Union (TEU) at Maastricht in February 1992 which, following a number of legal challenges and one referendum defeat, came into force in November 1993.

The TEU created the European Union. This consists of three pillars. The central pillar comprises the Communities—the ECSC, Euratom and the EEC—renamed the European Community. A number of amendments were made to the EC treaty. A citizenship of the Union was created, the principle of subsidiarity was expressly introduced into EC law, the powers of the Parliament were increased, and the legal mechanism for the introduction of EMU was inserted into the EC treaty.

The two other pillars concerned respectively common security and foreign policy (CSFP) and justice and home affairs (JHA). These remained outside the European Community pillar and in effect have the same character as any other international agreement between sovereign states.

The TEU was concluded for an unlimited period. Following the conclusion and ratification of the TEU, negotiations were rapidly concluded between the European Union and Austria, Finland, Sweden and Norway on accession. Following national referenda, the first three joined the European Union in January 1995, while Norway opted out (remaining part of the EEA).

1996: enlargement and the intergovernmental conference

The issue of effective institutional reform was not addressed to the satisfaction of many member states, such as Germany, the Netherlands and Italy, by the agreement at Maastricht. More qualified majority voting and more democracy in EC procedures are now considered vital by a majority of the member states. Efforts to obtain reform have been given a new impetus by the fall of the Berlin wall and the liberation of eastern Europe. The prospect of 20 or more member states in the early years of the next century provide an added sense of urgency to demands for removal of the veto and for more effective and accountable procedures.

The IGC convened at Turin in March 1996 marked the beginning of the latest treaty revision process, which is likely to lead to more majority voting, the transfer of powers from the intergovernmental second and third pillars to the European Community pillar, and a further increase in the powers of the European Parliament.